This Book Belongs to

_____

Christmas

Book 6

Content and Artwork by **Gooseberry Patch Company**

LEISURE ARTS
Vice President and Editor-in-Chief: Sandra Graham Case
Executive Director of Publications: Cheryl Nodine Gunnells
Director of Designer Relations: Debra Nettles
Publications Director: Kristine Anderson Mertes
Design Director: Cyndi Hansen
Editorial Director: Susan Frantz Wiles
Art Operations Director: Jeff Curtis
Senior Director of Public Relations and Retail Marketing:
Stephen Wilson
Licensed Product Coordinator: Lisa Truxton Curton

EDITORIAL STAFF
EDITORIAL
Senior Editor: Linda L. Garner
Associate Editor: Susan McManus Johnson

TECHNICAL
Technical Editor: Leslie Schick Gorrell
Senior Technical Writer: Theresa Hicks Young
Technical Writer: Shawnna B. Bowles
Technical Associate: Lisa Rickman

FOODS
Foods Editor: Celia Fahr Harkey, R.D.
Technical Assistant: Laura Siar Holyfield

OXMOOR HOUSE
Editor-in-Chief: Nancy Fitzpatrick Wyatt
Executive Editor: Susan Carlisle Payne
Foods Editor: Kelly Hooper Troiano
Photographers: Jim Bathie and Brit Huckabay
Photo Stylist: Ashley J. Wyatt
Test Kitchen Director: Elizabeth Tyler Luckett
Test Kitchen Assistant Director: Julie Christopher
Test Kitchen Staff: Kristi Carter, Nicole L. Faber, Kathleen Royal
Phillips, Jan A. Smith, Elise Weiss and Kelley Self Wilton

DESIGN
Design Manager: Diana Sanders Cates
Design Captains: Anne Pulliam Stocks and Becky Werle
Designers: Tonya Bates, Kim Kern and Lori Wenger

ART
Art Publications Director: Rhonda Shelby
Art Imaging Director: Mark Hawkins
Art Category Manager: Lora Puls
Lead Graphic Artist: Elaine Wheat
Graphic Artists: Ashley Carozza and Stephanie Hamling
Photo Stylists: Janna Laughlin and Cassie Newsome
Photographer: Russell Ganser
Publishing Systems Administrator: Becky Riddle
Publishing Systems Assistants: Clint Hanson, Myra S. Means
and Chris Wertenberger

BUSINESS STAFF
Publisher: Rick Barton
Vice President, Finance: Tom Siebenmorgen
Director of Corporate Planning and Development:
Laticia Mull Dittrich
Vice President, Retail Marketing: Bob Humphrey
Vice President, Sales: Ray Shelgosh
Vice President, National Accounts: Pam Stebbins
Director of Sales and Services: Margaret Reinold
Vice President, Operations: Jim Dittrich
Comptroller, Operations: Rob Thieme
Retail Customer Service Managers: Sharon Hall and Stan Raynor
Print Production Manager: Fred F. Pruss

Library of Congress Catalog Number 99-71586
Hardcover ISBN 1-57486-323-1
Softcover ISBN 1-57486-324-X

10 9 8 7 6 5 4 3 2 1

Christmas

Book 6

A LEISURE ARTS PUBLICATION

Christmas

Gooseberry Patch

Dedicated to our Gooseberry Patch family...thank you for sharing the magic of the holiday season with us.

How Did Gooseberry Patch Get Started?

You may know the story of Gooseberry Patch...the tale of two country friends who decided one day over the backyard fence to try their hands at the mail order business. Started in JoAnn's kitchen back in 1984, Vickie & JoAnn's dream of a "Country Store in Your Mailbox" has grown and grown to a 96-page catalog with over 400 products, including cookie cutters, Santas, snowmen, gift baskets, angels and our very own line of cookbooks! What an adventure for two country friends!

Through our catalogs and books, Gooseberry Patch has met country friends from all over the world. While sharing letters and phone calls, we found that our friends love to cook, decorate, garden and craft. We've created Kate, Holly & Mary Elizabeth to represent these devoted friends who live and love the country lifestyle the way we do. They're just like you & me... they're our "Country Friends®!"

Your friends at Gooseberry Patch

Mary Elizabeth ★ Holly ★ Kate ★ Spot

Table of Contents

Under the Christmas tree

Perfect Presents from the Pantry

Christmas cookery

A Circle of Memories

As you gather your circle of family & friends to celebrate, take time to recall the joys of Christmases past...and create new memories for younger generations to cherish. This may be the perfect year to begin an ongoing journal of wish lists, or you may want to craft festive covers for home videos, paint a memory box or begin a new tradition. Turn the page for more memorable ideas...and savor every moment of this magical season!

For a heartfelt family remembrance, fill a wreath with treasured mementos and ornaments, then add to it year after year to mark special events and milestones. How-to's for the Family Memory Wreath can be found on page 120.

These reversible frame-ups are perfect for tracking your children's growth each year! On one side, you can capture little handprints; on the other, record the date and display a snapshot of your child. Instructions for making the photo-backed Framed Prints are on page 120.

A fun countdown to Christmas! Get the family together during breakfast and think up 24 holiday activities, like making gingerbread cookies for classmates, dancing to holiday music, sledding or reading a Christmas story. Write each on a paper strip, link them together and then pull one off each day in December and do the activity together.

Give little ones a tiny Christmas tree of their very own decorated with a gumdrop garland, stuffed animals and candy canes...it's sure to make their holiday extra special!

Make a tree skirt to remember your children or grandchildren. Choose a plain fabric, put a fringe or border on to your liking. With chalk, trace each child's handprint. Have the mother or you embroider the hand, child's name and year. You can add to this forever!

— Pauline Williams

One never knows what each day
is going to bring. The important
thing is to be open and ready for it.
-Henry Moore-

A wonderful way to record the highlights of the season…ask family & friends to jot down their thoughts and memories of the season, past or present, in a Memory Journal that you can add to each year. *Turn to page 120 for the instructions.*

It's oh-so easy to paint a wooden box in holiday style, and it's the perfect place to store greeting cards, gift tags, snapshots or trinkets. To make your own Memory Box, see page 121.

A well ★ spent day brings happy sleep.
-Leonardo da vinci-

Get the whole family matching festive long-johns for silly but memorable Christmas pictures!

Surprise friends with a memory-making basket, complete with everything needed to record special moments…a blank scrapbook, decorative-edge scissors, photo corners and markers.

"Christmas! The very word brings joy to our hearts…there is still that same warm feeling we had as children, the same warmth that enfolds our hearts and our homes."

— John Winmill Brown

Make good use of a blank spiral-bound book…transform it into a family "Wishes" Journal (top photo; instructions on page 121). Those holiday home videos deserve special attention, and these festive Media Covers (instructions on page 121) are sure to please!

A great Christmas Eve tradition: Get everyone into their jammies, snuggle up with your special Story-Time Santa Blanket and read a favorite holiday book! To make the cozy wrap, see page 122.

Our traditional holiday game begins early in fall. Each member of our family picks a snow date…everyone trying to guess when we will get the first snow that covers the ground. One rule: no cheating by watching the weather channel ahead of time! Next, we all choose our favorite home-cooked meal. Choices vary from barbecue ribs to a huge pan of lasagna; however, as Mom, if I win, we go out to my favorite restaurant! With the addition of in-laws and lots of grandchildren, our family continues to grow and so does the excitement of the game for all of us.

— Sheila Dye
Ada, OH

Throughout the Christmas season I sing Christmas carols to my children as I tuck them in bed or rock them to sleep at night. There's never been a more beautiful lullaby than Silent Night sung softly in the darkness. This tradition takes me back to the time when my wonderful parents sang with our family. Although my parents are gone now, I feel them with me as I sing these special songs to their grandchildren and I hope that one day my children will enjoy this same feeling of closeness with their own children.

— Nancy Hauer
Rifle, CO

Are you traveling with little ones this Christmas? Make it fun for all. Wrap bows and garlands around the luggage rack of your car; take plenty of activity books, snacks, fruit juice, pillows and blankets.

Each Christmas Eve, after our girls are asleep, I put on some cherry red lipstick and give them each a kiss on the forehead. When they wake up Christmas morning, they find Santa's kiss. Each one then spends the day seeing whose kiss will last the longest!

— Kathy Larson
San Diego, CA

On Christmas Eve when my daughter was young, and I knew she was fast asleep, I carefully painted footprints across the kitchen floor leading to where she had left a plate of cookies for Santa and carrots for the reindeer. Each Christmas morning she was amazed at how those "elf" footprints were always there!

— Kristine Smith
Hampton, NJ

Did you know? There are towns named Santa Claus in Indiana and Arizona, one called Santa in Idaho and a North Pole, Alaska!

"Christmas is here,
Merry old Christmas,
Gift-bearing, heart-touching,
Joy-bringing Christmas,
Day of grand memories,
King of the year!"

— Washington Irving

Roast marshmallows over a fire in your fireplace…enjoy s'mores on a snowy evening.

As a child, it was a tradition to read "The Night Before Christmas" on Christmas Eve. After putting out a snack for Santa (and his reindeer too!), I would sit on my father's lap and he would read the story to me.

— Jean Quinn

I know a place
that's oh-so-sweet
at the end of
Gumdrop Street
Take a left on
Gingerbread Lane
You'll see the
House of Candy Canes
Designed by
Santa's little elves
with sweets inside
on every shelf!

All through the House

A soft blanket of snow, jingling sleigh bells, a cozy fire and lights twinkling on the tree…these are just a few of the sights and sounds of the season. Let Kate, Holly & Mary Elizabeth help you spread cheer all through the house with handcrafted ornaments and festive decorations for every room. They've also got oh-so simple how-to's for hosting a card-making party and a hearty holiday brunch!

Create a merry mantel! Spell out a festive greeting by embellishing wooden cut-outs with paint and pretty paper, then arrange them with greenery. Instructions for the Jingle Letters are on page 122.

Something Special

The simplest things can make each Christmas special…baby's first stocking, an ornament for a newly married couple or an Advent calendar to fill with little gifts. Instructions continue on page 122.

COUPLE'S BEADED ORNAMENT

Cut a 3" diameter circle from a photograph and a double-sided adhesive sheet. Use a craft glue stick to adhere the photo to a 3" diameter wooden cutout. Remove paper from one side of the adhesive; smooth onto photograph.

Remove the remaining paper from the adhesive; cover the adhesive with clear micro beads. Press the beads into the adhesive to make sure they stick and cover the adhesive completely.

Trimming to fit, glue 1/4" wide U-shaped lead came…the edging strips they use for stain glass…along the sides of the ornament. Glue the ends of a 6" length of nylon thread to the top back of the ornament for the hanger; glue a bow to the top of the ornament, then glue a charm to the knot of the bow.

Isn't it splendid to think of all the things there are to find out about?
- LUCY MONTGOMERY -

ADVENT COUNTDOWN

Paint a 16"x20" wooden frame to coordinate with your Christmas décor. Cut cardboard to fit in the frame. Wrapping and gluing the edges to the back of the cardboard, cover the cardboard with batting, then red fabric. Spacing evenly and gluing ends to the back, arrange and glue 4 lengths of 1½" wide ribbon on the covered board.

Use the envelope pattern from page 139 to cut 24 envelopes from Christmas cards or card stock; fold tabs under, then glue them along the ribbons. To number your envelopes, cut twenty-four 1" squares of card stock; use decorative-edge craft scissors to cut twenty-four ¾" squares from another color of card stock. Glue each smaller square to one larger

square. Stamp numbers 1 through 24 on the squares. Glue the numbers to the covered board beside the envelopes. Fill the envelopes with treats!

Plain glass ornaments become treasured tree trims when you decoupage them with traditional symbols of peace and happiness. Why not make a set to share with a young couple?

To craft your own **Symbolic Ornaments:** Cut designs from old greeting cards, wrapping paper or stickers; use spray adhesive to adhere them to clean glass balls (if the paper is stiff, it helps to clip the edges to help "ease" it around the curved surface). Add details with acrylic paint or paint-on snow, then sprinkle with glitter before the snow dries. Either hand-write or use alphabet stickers to spell out the meaning of each symbol on hang tags and tie to the ornament with ribbon.

The image of a rabbit brings HOPE for a bright future and a happy home.

A bird inspires JOY, both during the Christmas season and throughout the year.

Filled to overflowing, a fruit basket symbolizes GENEROSITY and kindness.

Pine cones remind us to be thankful for times of peace and PLENTY.

Messengers from heaven, angels bring GUIDANCE for our lives.

Santa, the children's friend, bears wishes of GOOD WILL to all.

Create·A·Card

CARD-MAKING PARTY INVITATION

For the invitations, purchase blank 5"x7" cards with envelopes. To decorate the front of each invitation, cut a 4¹/₂"x6¹/₂" and a 4"x5" piece of decorative paper. Photocopy the words (page 137) and Santa image (page 144) onto white card stock; cut out the letters and image. Arrange and glue the cut and photocopied pieces on the front of the card. Use a glitter pen to add a dash of sparkle to Santa's fur trims, then glue on 2 glittered snowflake cut-outs.

For the inside of the card, cut a 4"x4¹/₂" background from decorative paper; use decorative-edge craft scissors to cut a ³/₄"x3" and a 1¹/₈"x3" block from ivory card stock. Photocopy the words from page 137 onto card stock; cut out the words. Glue the background, words and blocks inside the card. Stamp your party information in the blocks. Glue on glittered and jeweled snowflake cut-outs as desired.

Get into the creative Christmas spirit! Invite a few friends over for a card-making party early in December. As the hostess, you'll need to buy enough supplies for each guest…the handy checklist on page 23 will help you get started. For refreshments, you can provide the beverages and ask each guest to bring a favorite snack to share.

The **BASICS:**
BLANK CARDS & ENVELOPES, TAGS & DECORATIVE PAPERS

Supply List

Hardware:
EYELETS & PAPER FASTENERS

LETTERING:
PAINT PENS, MARKERS, CRAYONS, PENS, COLORED PENCILS, STENCILS, STICKERS, RUBBER STAMPS & INK PADS, MAGAZINE CUT-OUTS

Tools:
STRAIGHT-EDGE & DECORATIVE-EDGE CRAFT SCISSORS, HOLE PUNCHES, WIRE CUTTERS, PAPER PUNCHES

EMBELLISHMENTS:
CUT-OUTS, STICKERS, CHARMS, WIRE SHAPES, PAPER QUILL APPLIQUES, SEED BEADS, MINI MARBLES, DIMENSIONAL SHAPES, BUTTONS, FABRIC SCRAPS, GLITTER

Trims: RIBBON, BRAID, PAPER FRAMES, RAFFIA, LACE, BORDER STICKERS

ATTACHERS:
GLUE, DOUBLE-SIDED TAPE, FUSIBLE WEB OR TAPE, WIRE, EYELETS

...and any other **STUFF** you'd use for **SCRAPBOOKING!**

Tickle
YOUR MIND.
- LINDSEY COLLIER -

spotty

Let us keep Christmas still a shining thing.

SANTA

merry merry merry merry merry merry

tidings of

Frosty

Here Comes Santa Claus

ho ho ho ho

to:

Happy Holly Days!

season's greetings

Merry Christmas

A JOLLY CHRISTMAS

HO HO HO

IT IS

So Simple

to create one-of-a-kind cards and tags. Before you get started, take a look at the supply lists on page 23. Our hints & tips will make it a breeze!

★ Have lots of cards you just can't throw away? Recycle them! Cut out images and glue them onto your new creations... you can reuse the words, too!

★ For a homespun look, use embroidery floss to sew on fun buttons.

★ If you don't like your handwriting, use rubber stamps or alphabet stickers! They come in all sizes and fonts.

HAVE FUN!

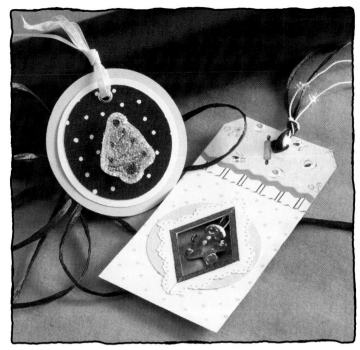

★ Don't make one card at a time... make FIVE so you'll have extras when you need one!

★ Add texture, use embossing powder or dimensional paint to draw over words... be sure to let it dry before sliding it in the envelope!

★ Use micro beads to add sparkle! They come in lots of colors, and are easy to attach using double-sided adhesive tape. Sequins & glitter are fun, too.

★ Draw around cookie cutters, then cut out the shapes. Use a double-sided adhesive foam piece to attach it to your card, and it will really "POP"!

Kids' Christmas Trims

Let the kids decorate their rooms for Christmas…use soft, cuddly velveteen to stitch up a colorful pillow sham and a jumbo-sized stocking for Santa to fill. Give them a little tree of their very own to trim, too!

Make the holidays Extra Special

for little ones…

★ HANG A STOCKING AT THE FOOT OF THE KID'S BEDS INSTEAD OF THE MANTEL … THEY CAN DIVE IN AS SOON AS THEY WAKE UP!

★ STIR UP SOME MEMORIES… INVITE GRANDMA & GRANDPA TO READ CHRISTMAS STORIES TO THE LITTLE ONES AND TO SHARE HOLIDAY STORIES FROM THEIR CHILDHOODS.

"Maybe Christmas, he thought, doesn't come from a store, maybe Christmas, perhaps, means a little bit more." —DR. SEUSS

Check out your local fabric store to find festive trims for the Tree Pillow Sham, then use them to finish the Oversized Stocking (instructions on page 123). Start a collection of handmade ornaments for the kids' tree…they'll have fun decorating Wooden Snowflakes with buttons and glitter "snow" (instructions on page 49).

Who says kids get to have all the fun? Mom & Dad can share in the merriment with whimsical pillows and Santa's Wreath. How-to's for the wreath and the buttoned-up Placemat Pillow can be found on page 124.

MARY ELIZABETH'S **QUICK CHRISTMAS PILLOWS!**

★ For 2 shams, you'll need 5 white tea towels, all alike. 2 of them will remain whole, for the pillow fronts... the other 3 will be cut.

★ Cut ⅓ off of 2 towels to make "A" pieces, like this:

A		A	

★ Now cut the remaining towel in half to make "B" pieces, like this:→

B	B

★ Hem all the cut edges.

★ For each sham, enlarge the pattern on page 147 to fit across one whole towel. Center the towel, right·side up, over the pattern; pin red chenille yarn along the word lines, then whip stitch it in place.

★ Pin one A and one B piece on a front piece... match wrong sides and overlap hemmed edges at center back, like this:→

A	B

Sew the pieces together 1" from the edges.
Insert a pillow in the sham, then....

take a little nap!

More Christmas fun! If your bed has tall bedposts, tie on big red bows and sprigs of holly or mistletoe. Arrange your collection of Santas across the dresser for a holiday parade. For festive sparkle, fill a shallow bowl with coarse salt and nestle in lots of tealights!

BATHROOM DÉCOR

Begin by making holly leaves...big leaves for the jumbo bells and top of shower and smaller leaves for smaller bells. Trace the leaf pattern on page 145 onto tracing paper. For each leaf, use the pattern to cut 2 leaves from green felt. Leaving a 2" stem, glue a length of wire down the center of one leaf, then layer the leaves together; work green *Running Stitches*, page 135, along the edges and down the center. For

each holly cluster, twist the wires of 3 leaves and a berry pick together.

Wire holly clusters and big silver jingle bells on an artificial greenery swag that fits over your bathroom mirror. String fluffy red chenille yarn on the swag just like you would garland on a tree. Now, hang the swag on the wall above the mirror.

To decorate the shower curtain, make 2 holly clusters for each jingle bell to go on your shower curtain. Tie a long length of red chenille yarn to the bell for the hanger, then wire one holly cluster to the bell. Tie the hanger to the shower curtain hook, then wire the remaining holly cluster onto the hook.

Put a vase filled with evergreens and berries in the bathroom for a fresh, Christmasy fragrance.

AAAAAH!

Buy a set of soft, fluffy towels in rich holiday colors, then sew on festive trims!

Farmhouse Kitchen Breakfast

Invite the whole family for Christmas brunch. The Country Friends® have some great ideas for kitchen and table trims…not to mention plenty of yummy breakfast goodies!

Jot down the day's menu on this festive Menu Board (instructions on page 124), or list activities you have planned for the day. And for an oh-so simple way to dress up the kitchen cupboards…just glue greenery and berry picks to mini grapevine wreaths, then use wide craft ribbon to hang them.

Make the place settings extra special with colorful holiday dishes and fleecy Mitten Placecards (instructions on page 124) to hold napkins and cutlery. Satisfying selections for a winter morning: Dish up hearty portions of Scrambled Egg Casserole and Grandpa's Fried Potatoes.

SCRAMBLED EGG CASSEROLE

A hit every time!

1/2 c. butter, divided
2 T. all-purpose flour
1/2 t. salt
1/8 t. pepper
2 c. milk
1 c. American cheese, cubed
1 c. cooked ham, cubed
1/4 c. green onions, sliced
12 eggs, beaten
4-oz. can sliced mushrooms, drained
1 1/2 c. soft bread crumbs, divided

In a medium saucepan, melt 2 tablespoons butter. Add flour, salt and pepper. Cook and stir until mixture begins to bubble. Gradually stir in milk; cook until thick and bubbly, stirring constantly.

Remove from heat. Add cheese, mix well and set aside. In a large skillet, sauté ham and onions in 3 tablespoons butter until onions are tender. Add eggs; cook and stir until they begin to set. Add mushrooms and cheese mixture; blend well. Pour into a greased 11"x7" casserole dish. Melt remaining butter; toss with one cup of bread crumbs. Spread over casserole. Sprinkle remaining dry bread crumbs over top of casserole. Cover and refrigerate for at least 2 to 3 hours or overnight. Bake, uncovered, at 350 degrees for 25 to 30 minutes. Makes 6 to 8 servings.

Diane Sybert
Athens, IL

GRANDPA'S FRIED POTATOES

Alongside eggs, any style, these potatoes make a great breakfast even better.

3 to 4 lbs. potatoes
1 lb. bacon
1 onion, chopped
seasoned salt to taste
salad seasoning to taste

Boil potatoes until tender; allow to cool, then peel and cube. Fry bacon and onion together in a large skillet; add potatoes and seasonings. Cook until golden. Serves 6 to 8.

Michele Olds
Avon Lake, OH

For lighter appetites, offer fruit-filled Empire State Muffins…they'll look even more appealing piled on a Decorated Cake Stand (instructions on page 124). Tangy, fruity Christmas Punch is a refreshing eye-opener.

CHRISTMAS PUNCH
Colorful and oh-so delicious.

2 qts. cranberry juice
juice of 4 lemons
1 qt. orange juice
1/2 c. sugar
2 qts. ginger ale
Garnish: orange slices and
    maraschino cherries

Mix together first 4 ingredients in a large bowl; pour into a punch bowl over ice. Add ginger ale. Garnish with orange slices and cherries, or freeze fruit in ice cubes to serve. Makes about 6 quarts.

Kathy Unruh
Fresno, CA

EMPIRE STATE MUFFINS
These make a meal in themselves and are so yummy!

1¹/₃ c. sugar
2 c. apples, cored, unpeeled and
    shredded
1 c. cranberries, chopped
1 c. carrots, shredded
1 c. walnuts or pecans, chopped
2¹/₂ c. all-purpose flour
1 T. baking powder
2 t. baking soda
1/2 t. salt
2 t. cinnamon
2 eggs, slightly beaten
1/2 c. vegetable oil

In a large bowl, combine sugar and apples. Gently fold in cranberries, carrots and nuts. Combine dry ingredients; add to mixing bowl and blend well to moisten. Combine eggs and oil, stir into apple mixture. Grease eighteen 2¹/₂-inch muffin tins and fill ²/₃ full. Bake in a 375-degree oven for 20 to 23 minutes; cool 5 minutes before removing from tins. You can also use 4-inch muffin tins and bake about 5 minutes longer.

Dorothy J. Carlson
Allegany, NY

If you collect milk glass serving pieces, fill them with greenery and berries…lovely in the kitchen or dining room!

34

MORNING PECAN CASSEROLE

The raisin-cinnamon bread and nutty topping give this a yummy taste.

8-oz. pkg. sausage patties
16-oz. loaf raisin-cinnamon bread, cubed
6 eggs
1½ c. milk
1½ c. half-and-half
1 t. vanilla extract
¼ t. nutmeg
½ t. cinnamon
1 c. brown sugar, packed
1 c. chopped pecans
½ c. butter, softened
2 T. maple syrup

Brown sausage patties on both sides over medium-high heat in a skillet; drain off fat and cut into bite-size pieces. Place bread cubes in a 13"x9" baking dish coated with non-stick vegetable spray; top with sausage pieces. In a large mixing bowl, beat together eggs, milk, half-and-half, vanilla, nutmeg and cinnamon; pour over bread and sausage, pressing sausage and bread into egg mixture. Cover and refrigerate 8 hours or overnight. In a separate bowl, combine brown sugar, pecans, butter and syrup; drop by teaspoonfuls over casserole. Bake at 350 degrees for 35 to 40 minutes or until center tests done. Serves 8 to 10.

Charlotte Peer
Newport, MI

F*or a country favorite, make up a batch of fresh, fluffy biscuits and milk gravy...add sausage, bacon or ham to make it even better!*

S*et out a variety of homemade jams for everyone to enjoy with muffins, biscuits or toast.*

COUNTRY BREAKFAST CASSEROLE

A small bag of frozen seasoned hash brown potatoes can be used instead of potatoes, onion and sweet peppers.

1 T. vegetable oil
4 potatoes, diced
1 sweet red pepper, diced
1 green pepper, diced
1 onion, minced
1½ c. egg substitute
1 c. milk
2 T. all-purpose flour
¼ t. pepper
4-oz. shredded Cheddar cheese
8-oz. pkg. breakfast link sausage, chopped

Heat oil in medium skillet. Fry potatoes in oil until golden. Add red and green peppers and onion. Mix egg substitute, milk, flour, pepper, cheese and sausage together in mixing bowl. Fold in hot potato mixture. Coat a 12"x8" baking dish with non-stick cooking spray. Pour potato mixture into baking dish. Bake at 350 degrees for 45 minutes. Makes 8 servings.

– Shirll Kosmal
Gooseberry Patch

"May you have the gladness of Christmas which is hope; The spirit of Christmas which is peace; The heart of Christmas which is love."
– Ada V. Hendricks

For a sweet & savory change of pace that's also easy on the chef, Morning Pecan Casserole is assembled the night before and then baked the next morning. Keep it warm in a cheery Casserole Cozy (instructions on page 124).

Start a Family Recipe Book filled with all the dishes from this season's family dinner, then add to it every year. Ask family members to hand write their most requested recipes, along with new favorites...memories to enjoy for a lifetime!

FAMILY RECIPE BOOK

Have your Christmas guests write their favorite recipes in this vintage-style recipe book...not only will you have a collection of all your favorite foods, but also original handwritten recipes from your family members to cherish forever.

For the covers, cut two 7¹/₂"x9" pieces from vintage fabric or linens, two 5¹/₂"x7" pieces of foam core board and two 5"x6¹/₂" pieces of card stock.

Center a foam core piece on the wrong side of each fabric piece. Fold and glue the corners of the fabric pieces diagonally over the corners of the foam core pieces. Fold the edges of the fabric pieces over the edges of the foam core pieces and glue in place. Center and glue a card stock piece to each cover piece, covering the fabric raw edges.

Stack the book covers and mark hole placements for eyelets; follow manufacturer's instructions to punch ¹/₄" diameter holes and attach ¹/₄" diameter eyelets.

For the pages, cut 5"x6¹/₂" pages from card stock. Using the holes in the cover as a guide, mark, then punch holes in the pages. Use clear self-adhesive photo corners to mount your 4"x6" recipe cards on the pages. Decorate the pages with stamps, stickers, charms or scrapbook embellishments.

Use 1" diameter binder rings to hold the book together. For the "spine," thread a length of ribbon through the rings, then tie it into a bow.

SUGARY PUMPKIN DOUGHNUTS

The dough is prepared the night before, so making these tasty old-fashioned doughnuts is a breeze.

3¹/₂ c. all-purpose flour
1 T. baking powder
1 t. baking soda
1 t. salt
¹/₂ t. cinnamon
¹/₂ t. ground ginger
¹/₄ c. butter, softened
1¹/₄ c. sugar, divided
2 eggs
²/₃ c. canned pumpkin
²/₃ c. buttermilk
¹/₂ c. brown sugar, packed
oil for deep frying

Sift together first 6 ingredients. Cream butter and ³/₄ cup sugar with an electric mixer in a large bowl. Add eggs, one at a time, beating well after each addition. Beat in ¹/₄ cup flour mixture; add pumpkin and buttermilk. Add remaining flour mixture, stirring until just blended. Cover and refrigerate 3 hours or overnight. Combine remaining sugar and brown sugar in a plastic bag; set aside. Roll dough to ³/₈-inch thickness. Cut out doughnuts; transfer to a floured surface and let stand 10 minutes. Heat oil in a large skillet; cook doughnuts on both sides until golden and cooked through, about 3 to 5 minutes. Place on paper towels to drain. While still warm, place each doughnut in the bag with sugar and shake to coat. Makes 2 to 3 dozen.

Paula Vento
Pasadena, CA

The aroma of Sugary Pumpkin Doughnuts will entice sleepyheads to join the celebration! For a frosty finish, serve Fruit-Filled Breakfast Cups…you can experiment with different combinations of fruit.

FRUIT-FILLED BREAKFAST CUPS

Every Christmas Eve afternoon, my family travels around our neighborhood delivering Christmas morning breakfast to our friends, neighbors and family. We include these fruit cups, homemade muffins and flavored butter.

2 10-oz. pkgs. frozen sliced strawberries, thawed
2 6-oz. cans frozen orange juice concentrate, thawed
2 20-oz. cans crushed pineapple
15¹/₂-oz. can mandarin oranges
¹/₃ c. lemon juice
6 bananas, sliced

Without draining fruit, combine strawberries, orange juice, pineapple, oranges, lemon juice and bananas in a large bowl; mix well. Spoon mixture into 5-ounce plastic serving cups. Freeze until firm; package in plastic airtight bags if needed. Remove from freezer 30 minutes before serving. Makes about one dozen.

Marcia Smith
Portage, MI

Try to beat the children getting out of bed on Christmas morning, then snap pictures of their sleepy, excited faces!

winter Wonderland

Create a winter wonderland with nostalgic treasures…a tabletop aluminum tree, family photos, pipe-cleaner snowflakes, handmade snow globes and other old-fashioned delights.

Pipe Cleaner Snowflakes

★ Start with 3 or 5 pipe cleaners.

★ Trim pieces off the ends... use 'em to twist, cross or bend into shapes:

diamonds teardrops

curls criss-crosses

★ Now stack and glue the shapes! you can curve some ends, add sequins & glitter to some, and add a pretty button center to each flake....

pretty!

VOILA! instant blizzard!

Craft tiny Photo Ornaments (page 124) to showcase vintage snapshots, and let everyone help shape Pipe Cleaner Snowflakes for the tree. Swag delicate eyelash trim and fine yarn over the branches and finish with silvery glass balls.

"I'm dreaming of a white Christmas."
— Irving Berlin

Create an enchanting arrangement of Jar Snow Globes on the coffee table or the mantel…you can enjoy them all winter!

JAR SNOW GLOBES

Remember being mesmerized by watching the gently falling snow in a snow globe…wondering "how the snow got in there" and "why doesn't it melt?" Recreate that enchantment by making one of these quick & easy globes using a small glass jar with a metal lid and a plastic ornament that will fit into the jar!

Begin by shaping oven-baked modeling clay "snow" around the lid…remember that when complete, the jar and lid will be upside-down, then follow the manufacturer's instructions to bake it. After the lid has baked and cooled, squeeze a big drop of clear-drying waterproof adhesive on the inside center of the lid, then press the bottom of the ornament into the adhesive and let it dry overnight.

The next morning you can put your globe together. Fill the jar with water, then add one drop of clear dishwashing liquid, 2 or 3 drops of mineral oil and iridescent glitter. Apply a thin layer of the waterproof adhesive around the inside threads of the lid, then twist the jar onto the lid and allow it to dry before turning right-side up.

"Oh the snow, the beautiful snow!
Filling the sky and the earth below!"

— J. W. Watson

Joy is that special sugar cookie recipe, long-yellowed by use and age. Joy is drinking cocoa from a Santa mug saved from childhood. Joy is searching for the perfect Christmas tree in the nearby forest and adorning it with sentimental ornaments. Joy is reading "Twas the Night Before Christmas" to kids of all ages. Joy is snow silently blanketing everything outside and the gathering of family & friends to share hugs and memories.

*— Debby Trapp
Baker City, OR*

FELTED-WOOL STOCKING

Wash a wool or wool-blend woven sweater in a washing machine set on the hottest water setting and the longest wash cycle; dry thoroughly in a hot dryer. (This will shrink the sweater to be really small…that's called felting.) You can then steam-iron the sweater to remove any wrinkles; just lay the sweater flat and wrong-side out with the neck unrolled on a flat surface.

Trace the stocking top and foot patterns, page 148, onto tracing paper, then cut them out. Matching arrows, tape the patterns together. Referring to Fig. 1 and starting with the top edge of the pattern along the neckline seam (the cowl collar will not be cut…it will be turned over the top of the stocking for the cuff), pin the pattern to the sweater. Allowing for a ¹/₂" seam allowance, cut out the stocking. Sew the edges of the stocking together, then turn the stocking right-side out.

This beautiful Felted-Wool Stocking also makes a great gift for a friend!

Fig. 1

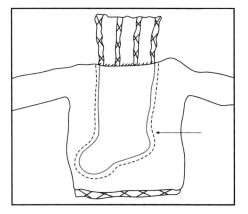

Fold the cuff down; use fabric glue to glue the flange of a length of decorative eyelash fringe along the inside bottom edge of the cuff. Use silver metallic pipe cleaners to make a **Pipe Cleaner Snowflake** from page 39; glue the snowflake to the cuff of the stocking. Stitch the ends of a loop of ribbon inside the cuff, along the heel-side seam, for the hanger.

Stitched with love, this huggable Stuffed Teddy Bear is an heirloom in the making! His arms and legs are jointed so you can pose him with your other collectibles.

Did you know…The first Teddy bears appeared in the early 1900's and were inspired by American President Theodore "Teddy" Roosevelt!

As the story goes, President Roosevelt traveled to Mississippi in 1902 to settle a border dispute. While he was there, his hosts offered to take him bear hunting, a popular sport of the day. During the hunt, President Roosevelt chose to release a bear cub rather than take it home as a trophy. The incident was related in a political cartoon in the Washington Post, and the entire nation became bear-crazy almost overnight!

Stuffed bears, known as "Teddy's Bears," were all the rage by 1906…society ladies were just as likely as children to be found toting the cuddly creatures, and a popular dance of the day, the "Teddy Bear Two Step" was accompanied by a song titled "The Teddy Bear's Picnic." Theodore Roosevelt even used a Teddy bear as the mascot for his re-election campaign!

When being together is more important than what you do, you are with a friend.
-CONNIE McMARTIN-

STUFFED TEDDY BEAR

- tracing paper
- heavyweight cream-colored felt
- 1/2 yard of plush fur fabric
- transfer paper
- heavy-duty carpet or upholstery thread and needle
- black 12mm safety eyes
- five 65mm hardwood disc joints
- polyester fiberfill
- black embroidery floss

Match right sides and raw edges, pin pieces together before stitching and use a 1/4" seam allowance for all sewing unless otherwise indicated…remember to leave openings as indicated on the pattern pieces until instructed to close. Clip curves before turning pieces right-side out.

1. Trace the patterns from pages 149 to 153 onto tracing paper; cut out. Use the paw and foot patterns to cut 2 shapes each from the felt. Place the fabric, fur side down, with the nap all pointing the same direction. With arrows matching direction of nap, draw 2 heads (one in reverse), one head gusset, 4 ears, 2 body fronts (one in reverse), 2 body backs (one in reverse), 2 arms (one in reverse) and 4 legs (two in reverse) on the fabric backing.

2. Cutting through the backing only; cut out each piece. Transfer aligning triangles; eye, nose, ear and joint placement marks; and opening marks from the patterns to the wrong sides of the pieces.

3. Sew the straight edge on each paw to the straight edge on each arm. Fold and sew each arm together, then turn right-sides out.

4. Sew sides and tops of each leg together. Easing to fit, sew foot pads to bottoms of legs. Turn legs right-sides out.

5. Beginning at nose point, sew a head piece to each side of the head gusset, then finish sewing the head pieces together from nose to front of neck. Sew 2 ear pieces together for each ear and turn right-side out. Slightly curving ears toward face and tucking raw edges to inside of ear, sew ears to the head. Follow manufacturer's instructions to attach the eyes. Trim the fur 1/4" from the neck edges; baste, then gather the neck tightly and tie threads to secure gathers.

(continued on page 125)

JOLLY GINGER BOYS

Who can resist the appeal of these jolly gingerbread boys! Re-live a little childhood fun…bake up a batch of spicy cut-out cookies to decorate, then pack them in a festive basket to share.

GINGERBREAD MAN BASKET

Paint the rim and band around a wooden basket white, then adhere checked border stickers to the bands. Trace the gingerbread man pattern, page 153, onto tracing paper. Use the pattern to cut 2 shapes from cookie-colored felt. On one gingerbread man shape, sew on small black buttons for the eyes and small red beads for the cheeks; sew a big red smile between the cheeks. Use green embroidery floss to tack on 2 star-shaped yellow buttons; tie the ends at the fronts of the buttons. Sew red chenille yarn into wavy trim across the legs and neck. Pin the 2 gingerbread men shapes together, then tack white bumpy yarn along the edges...be sure to catch both felt layers in the stitching. Fold and tack one arm over a small candy cane. Glue the gingerbread man to the side of the basket...line the basket with a piece of homespun. Finish off by piling yummy gingerbread cookies in the basket.

Let the kids help decorate an old-fashioned gingerbread house with icing and candies. To make pretty evergreen "shrubs," lightly brush rosemary sprigs with corn syrup and then dust with powdered sugar.

Decorate a tree with yummy gingerbread cut-outs...before baking, use a drinking straw to make a hole in each cookie that you can slip a length of ribbon through for hanging.

ask the smart cookie

Eenie, meenie, miney, moe... which pan is best for cookie baking?

★ The Smart Cookie is not aware of one.

Help! My cookies are yucky!

★ Select a cookie sheet 2" shorter than your oven for proper heat circulation.

★ Make each cookie the same size & thickness — for uniform baking & pretty little cookies!

Are you sure about those 52 cookies?

★ No.

★ Choose bright, shiny, heavy-gauge aluminum cookie sheets with very low or no sides for delicately browned cookies. Dark-colored sheets will cause cookie bottoms to over-brown.

Is there a law against eating 52 cookies in one sitting?

★ Here are a couple of hints: Don't use too much flour when making or rolling out cookie dough or you'll end up with dry, tough cookies!

★ Use jelly roll pans for bar cookies only. In addition, The Smart Cookie only uses insulated cookie sheets for certain cookies ~ cookies with high butter content tend to overbake on them.

★ Use a nice, big spatula to remove cookies from the baking sheet. Parchment paper on the pans work great, too.

Predict snowy weather with frosty outdoor décor! Oversize cargo tags add whimsy to the front door (see page 125 for the how-to's), and twinkling snowflakes light the way to your holiday festivities.

ELECTRIC SNOWFLAKES

For each snowflake, cut three 12" lengths from heavy-duty coat hangers. Wrap each wire length with white electrical tape. Crisscrossing at the center, place the 3 wires together to form a star shape; wire the centers together. Leaving plenty of room to hang the star and starting with the lights at the wall plug-in end of a 100 clear-bulb set of miniature outdoor lights on a white cord, thread lights up (try to rest one light at the end of each wire), then back down, each spoke of wire…use white electrical tape to hold lights in place. After each wire is covered, wrap the remaining lights around the center of the shape to form a ball. Tape the end of the lights up the same spoke as the hanger is on…this will allow you to plug several snowflakes together!

Make lacy snowflakes for your windows: Tape paper doilies to the inside of a window, then spray with water-soluble white paint and carefully peel away the doilies, leaving the lacy designs…they'll be easy to wash off later.

"…Snowflakes that stay
on my nose and eyelashes,
Silver white winters that
melt into spring,
These are a few of my
favorite things…"

— Oscar Hammerstein II

Family Fun Tree

Let the whole family join in the fun of trimming a tabletop tree for the playroom!

Great decorations for your family tree: Try hot-gluing checkers and dominoes to pom-pom ribbon for a garland...use the checkerboard as the base for the tree. Glue plastic letters together to spell everyone's name, tuck in Wooden Snowflakes and Retro Wooden Sleds, then add old-fashioned bubble lights.

Wooden Snowflakes

The perfect snowflake for kids to bring into the house ... guaranteed not to melt!

1. Glue 3 wooden craft sticks or craft picks together.

2. Paint them white.

3. Glue buttons to the snowflake.

4. Spray it with glue.

5. Cover both sides with "snowy" glitter.

6. Glue on a loop of nylon thread for the hanger.

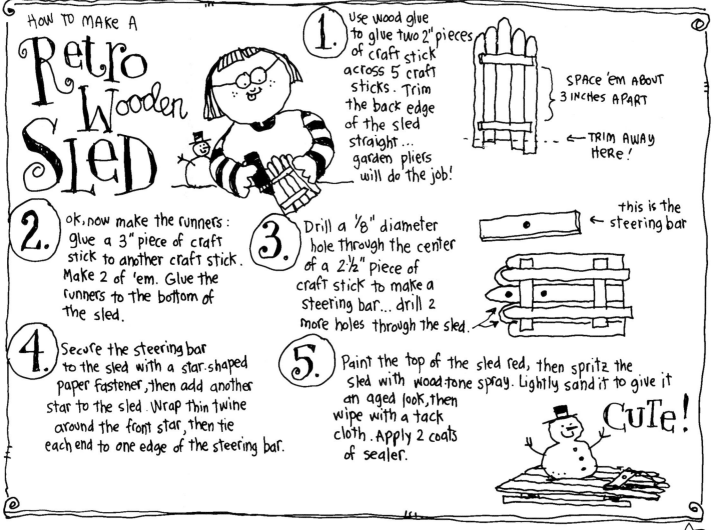

HOW TO MAKE A

Retro Wooden Sled

1. Use wood glue to glue two 2" pieces of craft stick across 5 craft sticks. Trim the back edge of the sled straight ... garden pliers will do the job!

SPACE 'EM ABOUT 3 INCHES APART

← TRIM AWAY HERE!

2. ok, now make the runners: glue a 3" piece of craft stick to another craft stick. Make 2 of 'em. Glue the runners to the bottom of the sled.

3. Drill a 1/8" diameter hole through the center of a 2½" piece of craft stick to make a steering bar... drill 2 more holes through the sled.

this is the ← steering bar

4. Secure the steering bar to the sled with a star-shaped paper fastener, then add another star to the sled. Wrap thin twine around the front star, then tie each end to one edge of the steering bar.

5. Paint the top of the sled red, then spritz the sled with wood-tone spray. Lightly sand it to give it an aged look, then wipe with a tack cloth. Apply 2 coats of sealer.

Cute!

Warm and Cozy

Create the coziest Christmas ever with soft, homey fleece decorations and accessories for the family room. You'll find fleece in lots of different colors and festive prints, so you can mix and match as much as you like! To make the Beaded Star Tree Topper and Fringed Garland, see page 126.

Heartwarming tree trims include square and heart-shaped Fleece Ornaments and whimsical Beaded Candy Canes, along with a cozy Pieced Tree Skirt. Craft a tiny grove of Fringed Trees and a matching Fleece Wreath. Instead of stockings, try hanging cute Personalized Felt Bags to hold little treats from Santa! Instructions begin on page 126.

"Christmas! 'Tis the season for kindling the fire of hospitality in the hall, the genial fire of charity in the heart."
— Washington Irving

My favorite Christmas memory is the year a big windstorm hit our town and the power went out. After lighting candles, we all gathered in front of the fire, and each of us shared our favorite Christmas memories. That night there were four generations laughing and crying together about Christmases past...I will never forget the closeness we felt.

— Rachel Keller

COZY FLEECE THROW

Most fleece is 58" to 60" wide...so you can make this throw from five ¹/₂-yard pieces of fleece. If you want your throw to be longer, you'll need additional yardage. Use long stitch lengths when sewing on fleece.

Cut four 13"x58" pieces from fleece...sew along each long edge ¹/₂" from edge. Overlap long edges ¹/₂", then zig-zag pieces together. (To avoid puckers along the seams, start each row of stitching from the same end each time.) Turn each outside edge ¹/₂" to the wrong side and zig-zag in place. Sew buttons along the seams.

For each tassel, cut a 3"x12" piece from fleece. Cutting to within ¹/₂" of opposite long edge and at ¹/₂" intervals, make clips along the strip for fringe. Roll the uncut long edge into a tight roll...sew together along the top coil, sew end in place. Insert the needle up through the center of the tassel, then through a wooden bead. Sew the tassel to one corner of the throw.

When I was growing up, my grandmother always gave us flannel pajamas for Christmas. Now that I have a family of my own, I always make sure my children have new flannel pajamas or nightgowns to wear Christmas Eve. I have even made them each a pair and flannel pants for my husband. It is the one gift they get to open on Christmas Eve. The pajamas always remind me of my grandmother.

— Carol Brashear
Myerstown, PA

Stitch a cuddly Fleece Throw and stack up plenty of Box Floor Cushions for comfy "floor-side" seats. Instructions for the cushions begin on page 127.

Under the Christmas Tree

Now that you've decked the halls and trimmed the tree, it's time for the best part of Christmas…crafting extra-special gifts! You can indulge family & friends with luxurious bath potions, treat Mom to a sparkly jeweled watch, delight Dad with a travel coffee mug for his morning commute or even make a fleece sweater for the family pet. Turn the page to find more ideas!

Luxurious accessories for the bath make great gifts. Close-up views and how-to's for the bath salts and fizzies, lip balms, facial scrub, lotion bars, candles, embellished towels, bathrobe, vintage bag and more begin on page 58.

Little Luxuries for the Bath

Everyone will think you found these luxurious potions at an expensive specialty shop…but they're really easy to make in your own kitchen! Each "recipe" makes enough for several gifts, so you can share indulgences like fragrant Bath Salts, Bath Fizzies and soothing Lip Balms with all your friends. The how-to's continue on page 128.

Essentials for a "home spa" gift package might include an inflatable bath pillow, natural sponges, a back brush, a bath tray, pretty scented soaps, after-bath splash and a CD of relaxing music or nature sounds.

When packing gift baskets, tuck in a little "bonus" for someone special…a certificate for a massage, a prepaid membership to the local health club or dinner at a fancy restaurant!

BATH SALTS

- 1 lb. Epsom salt
- 1½ t. essential oil (we used lavender)
- glass bottle with cork
- raffia
- hot glue gun
- small artificial flower
- card stock
- corrugated cardboard

Mix salt and essential oil together in a glass bowl, then pour into a glass bottle and seal with the cork. Tie several strands of raffia into a bow around the neck of the bottle; tie raffia into a bow, then glue a small flower to the knot of the bow. For the label, glue an oval cut from card stock to a rectangle of corrugated cardboard. Glue the label to the bottle. Makes one pound.

BATH FIZZIES

- 2 t. shea butter
- 4 t. essential oil (we used rose)
- 1 c. baking soda
- ½ c. cornstarch
- ½ c. citric acid
- 1 T. distilled water
- small candy or soap molds
- wax paper
- cellophane bag
- raffia
- craft glue stick
- card stock
- corrugated cardboard
- hole punch
- small artificial flower

Melt shea butter in a double boiler; add essential oil. Mix baking soda, cornstarch and citric acid together in a glass bowl; make an indention in the center of the ingredients. Drizzle the melted shea butter mixture into the indention and mix well. Add water and blend, mixture will fizz a little. After blended, pack firmly into molds (the firmer it's packed, the more it fizzes.) Let harden, then remove from molds onto wax paper. Allow to stand several hours before packaging. Makes about 48 small fizzies.

Place fizzies in a cellophane bag and tie closed with raffia; tie raffia into a bow. Thread a cardboard and card stock tag onto one raffia streamer. Glue a small flower to the tag to hold it in place.

Pamper a special friend…make these elegant Embellished Towels and microwavable Heating Pad (page 128); tuck them in along with a jar of oatmeal-brown sugar Facial Scrub and a handful of moisturizing Lotion Bars.

More Heavenly Concoctions to Share *(but keep a little for yourself, too!)*

Berry Bubbles

½ c. BABY SHAMPOO
¾ c. WATER
½ t. SALT
10-15 DROPS STRAWBERRY FRAGRANCE OIL

MIX SHAMPOO & WATER IN A BOWL. STIR GENTLY. ADD SALT AND STIR 'TIL MIXTURE SLIGHTLY THICKENS. ADD FRAGRANCE OIL. KEEP IN SEALED CONTAINER.

Merry Massage Oil

…SO RELAXING AFTER A LONG DAY OF HOLIDAY SHOPPING.

4 OZ. SWEET ALMOND OIL
½ t. PEPPERMINT FRAGRANCE OIL

BLEND OILS WELL IN A BOWL and POUR INTO A SEALABLE GLASS BOTTLE. SHAKE BEFORE USING.

LOTION BARS

- 1³/₄ oz. shea butter
- 2 oz. beeswax
- 1 T. liquid colorant
- 2 oz. sunflower oil
- 1¹/₂ t. essential oil
- gelatin or soap molds
- clear plastic stacking containers
  to accommodate mold-size
- small artificial flowers

Melt shea butter in a double boiler.
Add beeswax and colorant; melt
ingredients. Stir in sunflower oil
and allow to cool slightly; add
essential oil and mix thoroughly.
Pour mixture into molds and allow
to cool completely. Remove bars
and place in container. Add a label
and a tag, then embellish with
small flowers. Makes 6 bars.

FACIAL SCRUB

- 4 T. ground oats
- 3 t. brown sugar
- 2 T. plus 1 t. liquid aloe vera
- 1 t. lemon juice
- air-tight container

Mix ingredients together in a glass
bowl; stir until a smooth paste.
Scoop ingredients into an air-tight
container. Keep refrigerated when
not in use. Makes ¹/₄ cup.

*There is no delight in owning
anything unshared.*
— *Seneca*

Nothing makes a woman
more beautiful than
the belief
that she
is
beautiful.
-SOPHIA
LOREN-

Candle Creations

Fragrant, flickering candles create a soothing, tranquil mood and they're great for gift-giving, too! Try your hand at making your own Aromatherapy Candles...or, if you're short on time, craft Beaded Candle Bracelets and Votive Holders to dress up store-bought candles.

"It's impossible to describe the beautiful effect of firelight and candlelight...the smell of greens and woodsmoke is delicious. In the stillness of that first glimpse, one of the canaries will often trill into song."

— Tasha Tudor

AROMATHERAPY CANDLES

- 6½ oz. crème wax
- 9½ oz. candle wax
- 11 oz. beeswax
- large coffee can
- electric skillet
- craft stick
- lavender essential oil
- wax-coated candle wick
- pint or quart-size paper milk carton
- raffia
- dried lavender

Melt the waxes together in the can set in 1" of boiling water in the skillet…reduce heat to simmer and stir wax with a craft stick. After wax is melted, add 1½ teaspoonfuls of essential oil, then stir thoroughly. Cut a length of wick 1" longer than the height of the carton. Pour melted wax into the carton and allow to harden slightly. Insert wick at center of wax; allow wax to harden completely.

Carefully tear carton from around candle. If necessary, heat wax with a hair dryer and smooth with a soft cloth to remove any rough edges. Knot lengths of raffia around the candle, then tuck sprigs of lavender under the raffia. Remove raffia while candle is burning to reduce fire hazard.

BEADED CANDLE BRACELETS

Turn a plain pillar candle into an expensive-looking gift item by simply stringing assorted glass beads onto .5mm stretch cord lengths…the beaded cord should be long enough to fit the candle snuggly after the ends are tied together. To add dangles, thread several beads onto an eye pin, then loop the straight end; thread the pin onto the cord. Slide bracelets onto the candle…as the candle burns down, slide the bracelets down!

BEADED VOTIVE HOLDER

The perfect gift for teachers or special friends!

Wrap a piece of vellum around a glass votive; overlap and glue the ends. Crisscrossing at the front, place 2 **Beaded Candle Bracelets** around the holder.

Just for Mom

These stylish accessories are sure to please Mom! You can embellish the Lovely Trimmed Robe in a jiffy using extra-wide ribbon, and it's oh-so-simple to thread beads for an Elegant Timepiece. For a special evening, she'll enjoy a pretty Vintage Handbag. Instructions for the robe and bag are on page 129.

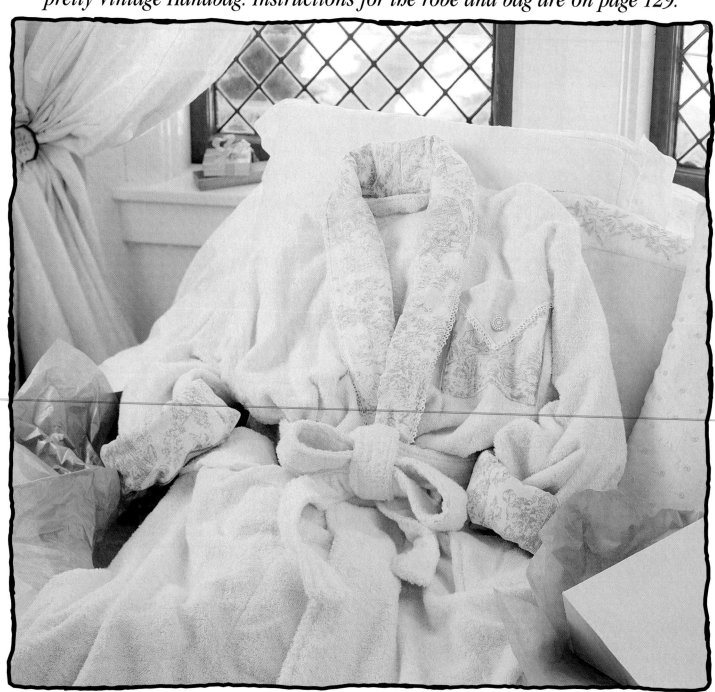

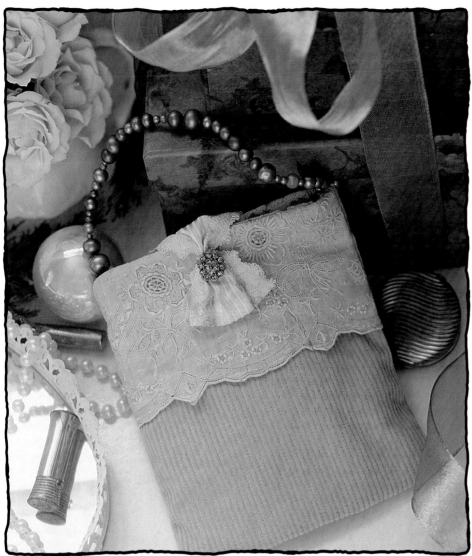

A couple of years ago, I gave my mom a "jar of thank-you's." I decorated a glass canning jar with stickers and ribbons and then filled it with about 100 strips of paper on which I had thanked my mom for all the little things she did to make my life wonderful. I included things like "Making orange juice popsicles for me and my friends," "Letting me have slumber parties," "Making snickerdoodles," "Encouraging me when I was away at college," "Adjusting my veil on my wedding day." Christmas morning, she read a few aloud and was so moved that she saved the rest to read on her own. She told me later that day that it was the best gift I had ever given her.

— Michelle Kirk
Hampton, VA

The heart has its own memory like the mind, and in it are enshrined the precious keepsakes, into which is wrought the giver's loving thought.
- Longfellow -

ELEGANT TIMEPIECE

Secretly measure your Mom's wrist; double that measurement and add 5". Cut a length of .5mm stretchable beading cord the determined measurement.

Thread the cord through the holes on one side of a watch face (available at craft stores)…make the cord even on both sides. Thread enough beads onto the cords to fit Mom's wrist, then thread one end through the holes on the opposite side of the watch. Tie the cords into a square knot and trim ends to about ¼". Apply a little jewelry glue onto the knot, then run the knot into the hole in a bead to hide it.

Just for DAD

Make this Christmas one that Dad will always remember! He'll be proud to display a Home Run Clock, page 130, on his desk…use photos of your children, or delight your own father with pictures of yourself as a child. The kids can decorate a handy Travel Mug, page 130, or craft a pocket filled with "Dad's Coupons."

dear old Dad
coupon card

YOU WILL NEED:

* TWO PIECES OF 8½" × 11" CARD STOCK
* ONE PIECE OF WHITE PAPER
* CRAYONS and A BLACK PEN
* GLUE STICK and WHITE CRAFT GLUE
* ALPHABET STICKERS
* A BUTTON
* 1½" × 4¼" PIECES OF PAPER FOR THE COUPONS!

1. FOLD ONE OF THE CARD STOCK PIECES IN HALF TO MAKE THE CARD.

2. CUT A POCKET-SHAPE FROM WHITE PAPER. GLUE THE POCKET TO THE OTHER PIECE OF CARD STOCK — CUT IT OUT A BIT BIGGER. COLOR THE POCKET.

3. GLUE THE EDGES OF THE POCKET TO THE CARD...LEAVE THE TOP EDGE OPEN! USE THE STICKERS TO SPELL "DAD'S COUPONS" ON THE POCKET, THEN GLUE THE BUTTON TO THE TOP.

4. WRITE FUN THINGS ON THE COUPONS; CHECK OUT OUR LIST AT RIGHT FOR IDEAS! DRAW DASHED LINES ON COUPONS. WRITE YOUR MESSAGE TO DAD ON THE INSIDE OF THE CARD.

5. PLACE COUPONS IN THE POCKET AND GIVE TO DAD TO REDEEM!

Don't settle for ho-hum gifts like socks, ties or cufflinks for Dad...find something he'll REALLY enjoy! Take your cue from some of his favorite activities and just use your imagination! Some neat ideas:

If he has a favorite sports team, pack a cooler with fun stuff like a team jersey or sweatshirt, pennants, a mug with the team logo, etc.

A golfer would enjoy a gift certificate for new equipment or accessories...tuck it in his stocking along with some new golf balls.

For a fisherman, fill a new tackle box with some of those fancy lures he's been wishing for...add a new filleting knife and a nice reel, too.

★ DaD coupon IDEAS!

one free crayon picture of you and me!

* ONE FREE BEAR HUG
* ONE FREE BUTTERFLY KISS
* ONE FREE DINNER
* ONE FREE BATCH OF COOKIES (WITH MOM'S HELP)

Fancy Footwork

Keep those tootsies warm & cozy with fancy footwear! Choose from Crocheted Slippers with fuzzy cuffs or multicolor Knit Socks (instructions begin on page 131).

CROCHETED SLIPPERS

Refer to Crochet, page 134, before beginning project.

Size Note: *Instructions are written for size Small, with sizes Medium and Large in braces {}. Instructions will be easier to read if you circle all the numbers pertaining to your size. If only one number is given, it applies to all sizes.*

SLIPPER SIZES

Small	9" (23 cm)
Medium	9½" (24 cm)
Large	10" (25.5 cm)

MATERIALS

Worsted Weight Yarn:
   White -
      $4^3/_4$\{5-5$^1/_4$\} ounces
      265\{280-290\} yards
      135\{140-150\} grams
      242.5\{256-265\} meters
   Red -
      $2^3/_4$\{3-3$^1/_4$\} ounces
      155\{170-180\} yards
      80\{90-95\} grams
      141.5\{155.5-164.5\} meters

68

Crochet hook as indicated below or size needed
  for gauge
  Size Small: size G (4 mm)
  Size Medium: size H (5 mm)
  Size Large: size I (5.5 mm)
Stiff bristled brush
Yarn needle

GAUGE: 16{14-12} sc and 16{14-12} rows = 4" (10 cm)

GAUGE SWATCH: 4" (10 cm)
With Red, ch 17{15-13}.
Row 1: Sc in second ch from hook and in each ch
across: 16{14-12} sc.
Rows 2 thru 16{14-12}: Ch 1, turn; sc in each
sc across.
Finish off.

STITCH GUIDE

SC DECREASE
Pull up a loop in next 2 sc on Side, YO and draw
through all 3 loops on hook (counts as one sc).
BEGINNING DC DECREASE (uses next 2 sc)
Ch 3, ★ YO, insert hook in next sc, YO and pull up a
loop, YO and draw through 2 loops on hook; repeat
from ★ once more, YO and draw through all 3 loops
on hook (counts as one dc).
DC DECREASE (uses next 3 sc)
★ YO, insert hook in next sc, YO and pull up a loop, YO
and draw through 2 loops on hook; repeat from ★ 2
times more, YO and draw through all 4 loops on hook
(counts as one dc).

(continued on page 130)

Family Friends

Don't forget your family's best friends during the holidays! Your dog will be the best-dressed pooch on the block in a cozy Doggie Sweater (see page 132) and kitty treats will stay nice and fresh in a whimsical Treat Keeper.

If you think dogs can't count, try putting three dog biscuits in your pocket and then giving Fido only two of them.

—PHIL PASTORET

SPOTTY BONES

KITTY TREAT KEEPER

Whimsical and practical, this gift is "purrr-fect" for the cat lover in your life!

Remove the lid from an airtight glass jar and set aside; place jar upside-down. Spray the outside of the jar with a frosted-finish spray paint.

For the lid, use enamel paints for glass to paint a dark red circle on the lid, then divide the circle into three sections and paint medium red stripes in different directions to resemble a ball of yarn. Paint one strand of yarn winding across the ball and leading down the side of the lid. Place the lid on the jar and continue painting the wondering strand of yarn around the jar as desired.

Use a black marker to trace the "Kitty Treats" pattern on page 156 onto white paper. Tape the pattern inside the jar at the front. Paint over the letters, on the outside of the jar, with black enamel paint.

Fill jar with kitty treats and present to your cat-loving friend!

Perfect Presents from the PANTRY

When you're searching for the perfect gift, look to your pantry for inspiration! No one can resist the appeal of goodies like homemade jam, holiday cookies, sweet breads and other classics. Along with incredible edibles, we've got a sleighload of tips for creating customized gift baskets, decorating jars to hold mixes and lots more creative packaging.

Everyone will want to be on your gift list when you share Best-Ever Sugar Cookies, White Chocolate Fudge, Oatmeal-Raisin Spice Cookie mix, Turkey Noodle Soup in a Jar, Christmas Marshmallow Pops and other great goodies!

oatmeal
raisin spice
COOKIE MIX

mixing bowl,
e mix, 3/4 cup
d butter, 1 beaten
teaspoon vanilla e
g ll. Shape int

TURKEY
NOODLE
SOUP

to the
URRAY KIDS

'Tis the
Season

It Must
Be
Christmas

Make
It
Merry

KIWI-CITRUS JAM

Perfect for morning toast or spread on bagels.

24 kiwi fruit, peeled and mashed
$^2/_3$ c. pineapple juice
$^1/_4$ c. lemon juice
3 apples, cored and halved
4 c. sugar
5 $^1/_2$-pint canning jars and lids, sterilized

Measure 3 cups mashed kiwi fruit; place in a heavy saucepan with juice and apples. Bring mixture to a boil; add sugar, stirring until dissolved. Reduce heat; simmer for 30 minutes. Remove apples and discard; pour mixture into jars. Wipe rims and seal with lids. Process in a boiling water canner for 10 minutes. Makes 5 jars.

PRALINE SAUCE

A sweet sauce filled with brown sugar and pecans. It's wonderful on ice cream or spooned over warm slices of pound cake!

$^1/_4$ c. butter, melted
1 c. brown sugar, packed
$^1/_2$ c. whipping cream
$^1/_2$ c. corn syrup
$^3/_4$ c. chopped pecans
1 t. vanilla extract

Combine butter, sugar and whipping cream together in a heavy saucepan. Over medium heat, stir until sugar is dissolved; add corn syrup. Continue to cook and stir until mixture thickens; add pecans. Remove from heat; stir in vanilla. Store in the refrigerator. Makes about 2 cups.

Carol Jones
Twin Falls, ID

*"Cookies we're baking,
presents we're wrapping.
Christmas is coming
and the days we're counting!"*

— Unknown

Homemade goodies are always welcome…add festive trimmings to plain baskets, then fill them with your best treats!

Surprise your favorite youngsters with a basketful of frosting-filled Best-Ever Sugar Cookies…package them in treat bags secured with colorful beaded wire. To decorate the Beaded and Wired Basket, see page 132.

COFFEE STIR STICKS

Each year I make gift baskets for my friends & family. I always include these stir sticks along with some flavorful coffee beans.

1 c. sugar
1/3 c. brewed coffee
1 T. corn syrup
1/4 t. baking cocoa
1/4 t. cinnamon
1/2 t. vanilla extract
12 wooden lollipop sticks
cellophane
ribbon

In a large saucepan, combine sugar, coffee, corn syrup, cocoa and cinnamon. Cook over medium heat until the sugar dissolves, stirring constantly. Continue to cook over medium heat for about 7 minutes, without stirring, until a candy thermometer reaches 290 degrees. Remove from heat and add vanilla; stir well. Pour into a greased 2-cup glass measuring cup. Working quickly, pour tablespoonfuls into circles on a greased baking sheet and lay a stick in each circle. Allow to cool at room temperature until hardened. When cooled, wrap with cellophane and tie with ribbon. Store in an airtight container. Makes one dozen.

Gail Prather
Bethel, MN

★ Find a flea market basket with not much personality — and give it a facelift. Spray paint it gold, rub off quite a bit of the paint for an aged look, and fill it with nuts & acorns.

Best Ever Sugar Cookies

a recipe from Susan Dixon
Topeka, KS

1/2 c. butter
1 c. sugar
1/2 c. oil
1 egg
1/8 t. salt
1 t. vanilla extract
2 1/2 c. all-purpose flour
1 t. cream of tartar
1 t. baking soda

Cream butter and sugar together in a mixing bowl; add oil, egg, salt and vanilla. In a separate bowl, combine dry ingredients; add to butter mixture. Form dough into one-inch balls and arrange on lightly greased baking sheets; flatten each with a fork. Bake at 350 degrees for 8 to 10 minutes. Makes about 3 dozen.

★ Put 2 cookies together with frosting in the middle and roll it in sprinkles!

Vanilla Buttercream Frosting

a recipe from Joanne Summers ★ Perry, GA

1 c. butter, softened
7-oz. jar marshmallow creme
1 c. powdered sugar
1 t. vanilla extract

Beat butter 'til creamy; blend in marshmallow creme. Add sugar & vanilla, beating 'til fluffy. Makes 3 cups.

Think "real" versus "toy" items for some children's presents, like real cookie cutters, rolling pins and measuring cups instead of toy versions. Receiving these is much more thrilling to a child and they last longer too.

— Vicki Wilkes

HOMEMADE PRETZELS

Just like they sell on New York City street corners.

2 pkgs. dry yeast
1¹/₂ c. warm water
2 T. sugar
3¹/₂ to 4 c. all-purpose flour
1 t. salt
1 egg, beaten
Kosher or coarse salt

Mix yeast, water and sugar in a bowl. Let sit approximately 10 minutes until frothy. (If it doesn't get frothy, your water was too hot and you killed the yeast; try again!) Add flour and salt. Flour your hands and work the dough until you have a soft, smooth (no longer sticky) dough. Break off a piece and roll it between your palms until you have a 12-inch rope. Twist into a pretzel shape; place on a lightly greased baking sheet. Beat the egg with one tablespoon water and brush each pretzel, then sprinkle with Kosher salt. Bake at 425 degrees for 12 to 15 minutes until golden brown. Eat pretzels warm, or reheat later in the microwave.

MUST-HAVE MUSTARD

Perfect with soft pretzels or served over smoked ham...a new family tradition.

¹/₄ c. coarse-grain mustard
¹/₄ c. Dijon mustard
¹/₄ c. dried basil
¹/₂ c. canola oil
3 T. brown sugar, packed
¹/₃ c. honey

Blend mustards and basil in a food processor until smooth; gradually blend in remaining ingredients. Cover and keep refrigerated. Makes 1¹/₂ cups.

Share a bag of soft Homemade Pretzels along with a jar of Must-Have Mustard in a rustic holiday basket (see So-Simple Baskets on page 77 for trimming ideas).

AUNT ESTHER'S CHOCOLATE CHIP COOKIES

Aunt Esther was a wonderful cook. I can't take these cookies anywhere without being asked for the recipe!

1 c. butter, softened
¹/₄ c. sugar
³/₄ c. brown sugar, packed
3¹/₂-oz. pkg. vanilla instant pudding
1 t. baking soda
1 t. vanilla extract
2 eggs
2¹/₂ c. all-purpose flour
2 c. chocolate chips
Optional: 1 c. chopped nuts

Beat together butter, sugar, brown sugar, pudding mix, baking soda and vanilla. Beat in eggs. Add flour and stir together. Stir in chocolate chips and nuts. Drop by heaping teaspoonfuls about 2 inches apart on an ungreased baking sheet. Bake for 9¹/₂ minutes at 375 degrees in a conventional oven or 10 minutes at 325 degrees in a convection oven. Butterscotch or chocolate instant pudding may be substituted for the vanilla pudding. Chocolate candies or butterscotch chips may replace the chocolate chips. Makes 4 dozen.

Cindy Caretto
Irvine, CA

GIVING ✶ Ideas:

GIVE YOUR GIFT TAGS & RECIPE DIRECTION CARDS A HOLIDAY SPARKLE··· GLUE A SPRINKLE OF **GLITTER** IN THE CORNERS OF TAGS & CARDS WITH EASY-TO-USE SPRAY ADHESIVE. CLEAR CRYSTAL GLITTER IS PRETTY, PRETTY, PRETTY. (HEY, GLITTER UP THAT TOTE BAG, TOO!)

A WHITE PAPER TOTE BAG WITH A RECIPE CARD GLUED ON THE FRONT WILL HOLD A MERRY MIX··· JUST ADD A PIECE OF WHITE TISSUE & A CASCADE OF WHITE CURLING RIBBONS··· a *wonderful* **WHITE** *Christmas gift.*

ALMOND-CHERRY CAKE

Because this cake needs to rest before serving, you can make it well in advance of any special occasion.

2 c. candied cherries, halved
1/2 c. blanched, slivered almonds
2 1/4 c. cake flour, divided
2 t. baking powder
1/2 t. salt
1 c. butter, softened
1 c. sugar
1 t. almond extract
4 eggs
1/3 c. milk

Combine cherries, almonds and 1/2 cup flour in a bowl; mix until fruit is well coated. In a separate bowl, sift together remaining flour, baking powder and salt; set aside. Cream butter, sugar and almond extract until light and fluffy. Add eggs, one at a time, beating well after each addition. Alternately add flour mixture and milk to creamed mixture. Stir in floured fruit and nuts; spread into 2 greased and floured 8 1/2" x 4 1/2" loaf pans. Bake at 300 degrees for 45 to 50 minutes or until inserted toothpick comes out clean. Cool in pan for 10 minutes; turn onto a wire rack to cool completely. Wrap in aluminum foil and store in a cool place for several days to allow flavors to blend. Makes 2 loaves.

SO-SIMPLE BASKETS

You can add basket liners, berry garland, big bows and handmade tags to purchased baskets for quick & easy gift giving. (See page 133 for *tag how-to's* and page 134 for *Bow Basics*.) Tuck in artificial greenery for a seasonal splash. A neat trick for jar labels is to place a ribbon tie between the card stock layers when making the label, then tie the label to the jar.

You can bake plenty of Almond-Cherry Cakes ahead of time and freeze to have on hand for quick holiday gifts…tuck them into So-Simple Baskets for delivery.

TURKEY NOODLE SOUP IN A JAR

Make several batches to keep on hand for last-minute gifts during the holiday season.

1/4 c. dried red lentils
2 T. dried, minced onion
1 T. plus 1 1/2 t. chicken bouillon granules
1/2 t. dill weed
1/8 t. celery seed
1/8 t. salt
1/8 t. garlic powder
1 bay leaf
1 c. egg noodles, uncooked

In a one-pint, wide-mouth jar, layer ingredients in the order listed. Seal jar and attach cooking instructions.

Instructions: Bring 8 cups water to a boil in a large saucepan; stir in jar contents. Cover, reduce heat and simmer 15 minutes. Remove and discard bay leaf. Stir in a 10-ounce package frozen mixed vegetables and 2 cups cooked and diced turkey. Cook 5 minutes until meat and vegetables are tender. Makes 10 cups.

DECORATED JARS

Spiff up your gift mix jars. Add a decorative lid cover...simply cut a circle of scrapbook paper to fit the lid. You can hand letter, stamp or sticker on the recipe name. Border stickers and fabric trim make quick accents around the lid's edge. And most importantly, add a custom label or tag with the cooking instructions. Use raffia to tie on fun charms or the tag.

Ready-to-fix mixes make it easy for friends to prepare yummy treats...and since you don't have to do the cooking, they save time for you too!

Make your gift mixes extra special...layer the ingredients for Oatmeal-Raisin Spice Cookies or Turkey Noodle Soup in colorfully Decorated Jars.

OATMEAL-RAISIN SPICE COOKIES

An easy-to-make gift mix! Attach a gift card with the baking directions.

3/4 c. brown sugar, packed
1/2 c. sugar
3/4 c. raisins
2 c. quick-cooking oats, uncooked
1 c. all-purpose flour
1 t. cinnamon
1/4 t. nutmeg
1 t. baking powder
1/2 t. salt

In a one-quart, wide-mouth jar, layer brown sugar, sugar, raisins and oats, packing down tightly in between each layer. Sift together flour, cinnamon, nutmeg, baking powder and salt; layer over oats. Seal jar and give a gift card with baking instructions.

Instructions: Combine dry ingredients in a large mixing bowl; add 3/4 cup softened butter, 1 beaten egg and 1 teaspoon vanilla extract, mixing well. Shape into walnut-size balls; place on greased baking sheets. Bake at 350 degrees for 15 minutes or until edges are golden brown. Cool on wire racks. Makes about 3 dozen.

Kim Robertson
South Hill, VA

BROWNIE SAND CASTLES MIX

Who doesn't love brownies? This mix will be a welcome gift!

1/2 c. chopped pecans
1/2 c. semi-sweet chocolate chips
1/3 c. flaked coconut
2/3 c. brown sugar, packed
3/4 c. sugar
1/3 c. baking cocoa
1 1/2 c. all-purpose flour

In a one-quart, wide-mouth jar, layer the first 6 ingredients in the order listed, packing each layer down well. After adding the cocoa, use a paper towel to wipe the inside of the jar

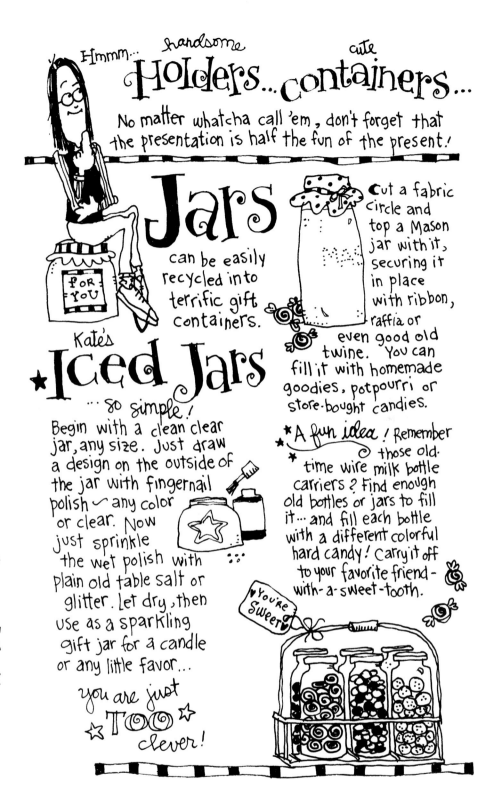

Holders... containers...

No matter whatcha call 'em, don't forget that the presentation is half the fun of the present!

Jars can be easily recycled into terrific gift containers.

Cut a fabric circle and top a Mason jar with it, securing it in place with ribbon, raffia or even good old twine. You can fill it with homemade goodies, potpourri or store-bought candies.

Kate's ★Iced Jars

... so simple!

Begin with a clean clear jar, any size. Just draw a design on the outside of the jar with fingernail polish ⌒ any color or clear. Now just sprinkle the wet polish with plain old table salt or glitter. Let dry, then use as a sparkling gift jar for a candle or any little favor...

you are just ☆ TOO ☆ clever!

*A fun idea! Remember those old-time wire milk bottle carriers? Find enough old bottles or jars to fill it... and fill each bottle with a different colorful hard candy! Carry it off to your favorite friend-with-a-sweet-tooth.

to remove any cocoa from the sides; add flour. Cover filled jar with the lid and tie on a gift card with the instructions.

Instructions: Cream together 2 eggs, 2/3 cup oil, 1 teaspoon vanilla extract and 1 teaspoon almond extract. Stir in brownie mix and

beat until well blended. Spread batter into an oiled 8"x8" baking dish. Bake at 350 degrees for 30 to 40 minutes, or until the center tests done. Cool on a wire rack. Makes approximately 1 1/2 dozen.

Wendy Paffenroth
Pine Island, NY

What smells better than waking up to

Gingerbread Pancakes?

a recipe from Karyn Kyllo ✷ Spokane, WA

POP A BAG·FULL OF THIS YUMMY MIX INSIDE AN APRON POCKET ∽ COPY THE RECIPE CARD ON PAGE 144; ADD THE RECIPE AND A WOODEN SPOON!

3/4 c. WHOLE·WHEAT FLOUR
1/4 c. ALL·PURPOSE FLOUR
1 t. BAKING POWDER
1/4 t. SALT
3 T. BROWN SUGAR, PACKED
1/2 t. GROUND GINGER
1/4 t. CINNAMON
1/8 t. GROUND CLOVES

COMBINE ALL INGREDIENTS AND PLACE IN A SELF·SEALING PLASTIC BAG. ATTACH INSTRUCTIONS.

CHRISTMAS BISCOTTI MIX

I like to give this mix with a baking sheet and holiday pot holders.

3/4 c. dried cranberries or cherries
3/4 c. shelled green pistachios
2 c. all-purpose flour
1/2 t. cardamom
2 t. baking powder
2/3 c. vanilla sugar

Layer all ingredients in a one-quart, wide-mouth canning jar, packing down tightly after each addition. Secure lid and attach a gift tag with baking instructions.

Baking Instructions: Beat 1/3 cup butter in a large mixing bowl at medium speed for 30 seconds. Add 2 eggs and beat at medium speed until well combined. Stir in jar of mix until blended. Form dough into two 9"x2" loaves on a lightly greased baking sheet. Bake at 375 degrees for 25 to 30 minutes; cool on sheet for one hour. Cut each loaf into slices 1/2 inch thick. Arrange slices on baking sheets and bake at 325 degrees for 8 minutes; turn each over and bake 8 to 10 additional minutes or until dry and crisp. Cool on a wire rack. Makes 2 to 3 dozen.

Ellie Brandel
Clackamas, OR

Homemade vanilla sugar couldn't be easier! Just pour 4 cups of sugar into a one-quart jar. Slice one vanilla bean in half lengthwise and add both halves to the sugar, then put the lid on the jar and let it sit for 2 to 3 weeks. Vanilla sugar adds a delightful flavor to coffee or cereal…or substitute it for regular sugar in your favorite baking recipes.

For a Christmas morning treat, slip a bag of Gingerbread Pancake mix into the pocket of a Holiday Apron (page 133). Be sure to include the recipe!

SLOPPY JOE MIX

Surprise coaches, teachers or scout leaders with this mix!

2 T. dried, minced onion
2 T. dried green pepper flakes
1½ t. salt
2 t. cornstarch
¼ t. dry mustard
1 t. celery seed
½ t. chili powder
½ t. garlic salt

Mix ingredients together until well blended; store in an airtight container. Attach instructions. Makes about 5 tablespoons.

Instructions: Brown one pound ground beef in a skillet; drain. Add seasoning mix, ½ cup water and an 8-ounce can of tomato sauce; bring to a boil. Reduce heat; simmer for 10 minutes, stirring often. Spoon onto buns to serve. Makes 6 servings.

PARMESAN-GARLIC POPCORN SPICE

Everyone in my office seems to be snacking on popcorn every afternoon. I gave this spice to them last year and they loved it!

½ c. grated Parmesan cheese
2 t. salt
1 t. dried tarragon
1 t. garlic powder
1 t. dried parsley

Combine all ingredients in a small bowl; stir until well blended. Store in an airtight container. Give with instructions for serving. Makes ½ cup mix.

Serving Instructions: Melt ¼ cup butter in a small saucepan over low heat. Stir in one tablespoon popcorn spice. Pour over 3 cups popped popcorn; stir well.

Bonnie Weber
West Palm Beach, FL

Need a bunch of little gifts for co-workers?

Neat Ideas from Mary Elizabeth

★ Cut shapes from felt (stars, holly leaves, gingerbread men)... punch a hole near the edge, glue on beads or sequins, then tie onto candy canes with a ribbon.

★ Make a double batch of yummy cocoa mix... pack 1 cup per person in a resealable bag and drop it in a rubber-stamped paper lunch sack. Don't forget the mixing instructions!

★ **Great for club members!**

Pepperminty Cocoa

a good idea from Jen Sell ★ Farmington, MN

3 c. powdered milk
1¼ c. sugar
½ c. baking cocoa
8 to 10 peppermint candies, crushed
⅛ t. salt

Stir all ingredients together and store in a wide-mouth, one-quart canning jar or airtight container.

Make a cute and yummy gift! Glue a whole, round peppermint on top of the jar lid.... tie a scrap of red & white homespun 'round the jar neck and slip a candy cane in the knot... and glue a copy of the instructions on page 144 on the jar!

Kitchen Classics

You can't go wrong with classic sweet breads, snack mixes and candies! We've got a great selection of old favorites, along with a few new flavors.

RAISIN-APPLE BREAD

Wrap the bread in plastic and tie a bow around the ring to make a wreath.

3 c. all-purpose flour
2½ c. sugar
2 t. cinnamon
1½ t. salt
1½ t. baking soda
½ t. cloves
½ t. baking powder
1¼ c. oil
4 eggs, lightly beaten
1 T. and 1 t. vanilla extract
3 c. apples, cored, peeled and diced
⅔ to 1 c. raisins
1 c. walnuts, chopped

Beat first 10 ingredients together for about 2 minutes. Stir in apples, raisins and nuts. Bake in 2 greased and floured 1-quart ring pans at 325 degrees for 45 to 55 minutes or until toothpick comes out clean.

CHOCOLATE-PEANUT POPCORN

Milk chocolate and popcorn...all you need is a good movie!

12 c. popped popcorn
2¼ c. salted peanuts
1¾ c. milk chocolate chips
1 c. corn syrup
¼ c. butter

Combine popcorn and nuts in a greased roasting pan; set aside. In a heavy saucepan, melt together chocolate chips, corn syrup and butter, stirring constantly. Bring to a boil; pour over popcorn, tossing well to coat. Bake at 300 degrees for 30 to 40 minutes, stirring every 10 minutes. Remove from oven, stir and allow to cool slightly in pan. Cool completely on a baking sheet lined with wax paper. Store in an airtight container. Makes 14 cups.

You won't find this wreath hanging on the front door! Decorate a ring of deliciously moist, spicy Raisin-Apple Bread with a cheery bow.

SPICY TEX-MEX MIX

A snacky treat with a Mexican twist.

2¹/₂ c. lightly salted peanuts
3 c. corn chips
3 c. shredded wheat cereal
2¹/₂ c. lightly salted pretzels
1¹/₄-oz. pkg. taco seasoning mix
¹/₄ c. butter, melted

Combine all ingredients in a large bowl; toss well to coat. Store in an airtight container. Makes 11 cups.

CELEBRATION BEAN SOUP

It's a party in every jar!

12 1-pt., wide-mouth jars and lids
2 lbs. dried baby lima beans
2 lbs. dried lentils
2 lbs. dried red lentils
2 lbs. dried black-eyed peas
2 lbs. dried pinto beans
2 lbs. dried white beans
2 lbs. dried navy beans
2 lbs. dried kidney beans
12 cubes chicken bouillon
12 bay leaves

In each jar, layer ¹/₄ cup of each type of bean. Place one bouillon cube and one bay leaf on top of the beans in each jar. Seal lid and attach cooking instructions. Makes 12 jars.

Instructions: Set aside bouillon cube and bay leaf. Rinse beans and place in a large pot. Add 6 to 8 cups hot water; bring to a rapid boil and boil 2 minutes. Remove from heat. Cover and let stand one hour. Drain water and rinse beans. Add 6 cups water, a 14-ounce can chopped tomatoes, bay leaf and bouillon cube. Simmer over medium-low heat until beans are tender, about 2 hours. Season with salt and pepper to taste. Makes 4 servings.

It's fun & easy to fill nifty gift cones with Spicy Tex-Mex Mix, Celebration Bean Soup mix or other treats…tie with ribbon and add colorful tags.

Nifty Gifties!

THOSE CLEAR PLASTIC BAGS THAT YOU USE TO PIPE ICING ALSO MAKE FUN HOLDERS FOR HOLIDAY GOODIES! FILL THEM WITH...

* Red, Green & yellow Jelly beans (layered or all mixed up)
* Your favorite caramel corn
* Layers of different dried fruits
* mixed nuts   * snack mixes
* Red & green sugared jellied candies
* and Kate says... *Chocolates!*

FINISH YOUR NIFTY GIFTIES WITH RUBBER-STAMPED TAGS!

CHRISTMAS MARSHMALLOW POPS
A fun treat for a holiday party.

1 c. semisweet chocolate chips
2 T. shortening
peppermint sticks or canes
10-oz. pkg. large marshmallows
chopped nuts, decorating sugar
 and candy sprinkles

In a 2-cup glass measure, microwave chocolate chips and shortening at 50% power for 1½ to 3 minutes or until chips are shiny and soft; stir until smooth. For each marshmallow pop, insert a peppermint stick into each marshmallow. Dip marshmallow into melted chocolate; let stand, upright, 1 to 3 minutes or until chocolate is very slightly set. Sprinkle with nuts, sugar or sprinkles; stand upright until chocolate is completely set. Store in a covered container. Makes about 50 pops.

Indulge a friend with a Joy Box (page 133) filled with squares of incredibly creamy White Chocolate Fudge. You can use your imagination to decorate fun Christmas Marshmallow Pops (right).

I remember the Christmas season, with its blustery nights, when I would find my precious mother in the kitchen making fudge and hearing the sound of dancing popcorn on the stove. My two sisters and I would linger at Mom's side to see which one of us would get the privilege of licking the chocolate off the old wooden spoon…the chocolate aroma in the air, mixed with the scent of popcorn, just made our tiny mouths water for the tasty treats! Our evenings together were magical as we tasted the delights of tempting snacks, and it gave Mom & Dad time to hear the three of us tell them our Christmas wishes and dreams. Time is such a fleeting thing. Grab every wonderful moment and each loving memory, then hold them in your heart.

— Thais Menges
Three Rivers, MI

WHITE CHOCOLATE FUDGE
Just right for tucking in holiday tins!

8-oz. pkg. cream cheese, softened
4 c. powdered sugar
1½ t. vanilla extract
12 oz. white chocolate
¾ c. chopped walnuts

Cream together cream cheese, sugar and vanilla until smooth. Melt chocolate in a double boiler, then stir into cream cheese mixture. Fold in walnuts and spread into a greased 8"x8" baking pan. Chill until ready to serve and cut into squares.

Jo Ann

CHRISTMAS CHEESE BALLS
Try shaping these into mini bite-size cheese balls, too.

2 8-oz. pkgs. cream cheese
¼ c. onion, chopped
¼ c. green pepper, diced
½ c. crushed pineapple
¼ c. maraschino cherries, diced
1 t. garlic salt
1 t. onion salt
1 T. Worcestershire sauce
1 t. seasoned salt
1 c. chopped pecans
2 T. fresh parsley, chopped
red and green maraschino
    cherries, chopped

Blend cream cheese, onion, green pepper, pineapple, cherries, garlic salt, onion salt, Worcestershire sauce and seasoned salt together. Shape into 3 balls. Roll in pecans and parsley. Top with cherries.

Karen Wardle
Salt Lake City, UT

the Country Friends' YUM!

Caramel Apple Popcorn Balls
~ OLD-FASHIONED FUN! ~

1 . ½ QTS. POPPED POPCORN
2 c. CRISPY RICE CEREAL
½ c. CHOPPED DRIED APPLES
14 . OZ . PKG. CARAMELS,
        UNWRAPPED

2 T. WATER
2 T. BUTTER
1 t. CINNAMON

★

TOSS POPCORN, CRISPY RICE CEREAL and APPLES TOGETHER IN A LARGE BOWL; SET ASIDE. PLACE CARAMELS, WATER and BUTTER IN A MEDIUM SAUCEPAN; HEAT OVER LOW HEAT UNTIL CARAMELS ARE MELTED, STIRRING UNTIL SMOOTH. ADD CINNAMON; REMOVE FROM HEAT. POUR OVER POPCORN MIXTURE; TOSS TO COAT. LET COOL ABOUT 5 MINUTES; SHAPE INTO BALLS USING SLIGHTLY DAMP and BUTTERED HANDS. ARRANGE ON WAX PAPER 'TIL FIRM. WRAP THE POPCORN BALLS INDIVIDUALLY IN PLASTIC WRAP. MAKES 8.

Decorate a tree in your back yard with strings of popcorn and cranberries...cheery garlands that the birds will love, too!

Dip half (or all!) of a batch of homemade sugar cookies in melted chocolate for a simply irresistible chocolatey treat!

"The only things we ever keep are what we give away."

— Louis Ginsberg

Christmas Cookery

Just ask Kate, Holly or Mary Elizabeth, and they'll tell you that the best Christmas magic comes from the kitchen! We all look forward to special holiday fare...tempting cookies and candies, appealing appetizers and savory snacks, creative casseroles and main dishes...along with hearty helpings of love and laughter shared with family & friends.

An English tradition, old-fashioned Prime Rib & Yorkshire Pudding will satsify the heartiest holiday appetites. Don't be surprised if your family likes this dish better than the usual holiday ham!

THE MaiN EvenT

Whether your big celebration is on Christmas Day, Christmas Eve or New Year's, make the family meal an event to remember! Try adding some new dishes to your menu…you may be creating new traditions.

Wild Rice Stuffing

PRIME RIB & YORKSHIRE PUDDING

Savory Yorkshire pudding is a traditional English treat…its texture is more like a popover or soufflé than a pudding!

Prime Rib:
1 c. all-purpose flour
1 t. salt
pepper to taste
9¹/₂-lb. boneless rib roast

Combine flour, salt and pepper; coat roast and place in a shallow roasting pan. Bake at 450 degrees 10 minutes; reduce oven temperature to 325 degrees and bake 2¹/₂ hours longer or until meat thermometer registers 140 degrees. Place roast on a carving board, reserving drippings for Yorkshire Pudding. Cover roast and let stand 5 to 10 minutes or until thermometer reaches 145 degrees (medium rare) before carving. Makes 14 to 16 servings.

Yorkshire Pudding:
6 T. roast drippings
¹/₂ c. milk
¹/₂ c. water
2 eggs
¹/₄ c. all-purpose flour
³/₄ t. salt

Place drippings in an 11"x17" baking dish; put in a 425-degree oven for 5 minutes. Whisk remaining ingredients until smooth; pour over hot drippings and bake 20 minutes or until puffed and brown.

WILD RICE STUFFING

Dates and crunchy almonds make this stuffing recipe special!

1¹/₃ c. wild rice
2 T. butter
2 c. onion, chopped
1 c. carrots, grated
1 c. green pepper, chopped
6 c. herb-seasoned stuffing mix
1 c. slivered almonds
¹/₂ c. fresh parsley, chopped
10-oz. pkg. pitted dates, chopped
1¹/₂ t. dried rosemary
1¹/₂ t. dried thyme
1¹/₂ t. dried sage
3 c. chicken broth

Prepare rice according to package directions; set aside. Combine butter, onion, carrots and pepper in a saucepan and sauté until onion is transparent; remove from heat. Blend in remaining ingredients; stir in rice. Spoon stuffing into a greased 13"x9" baking pan and bake at 325 degrees, covered, for 45 minutes. Remove cover and bake an additional 15 minutes. Makes 10 cups.

Vickie

TASTY POPPY SEED DRESSING

A favorite when poured on a salad of Romaine lettuce, strawberries, raspberries and kiwi.

1 c. banana, mashed
¹/₂ c. sour cream
¹/₂ c. mayonnaise
¹/₂ c. sugar
1 T. lemon juice
1 t. dry mustard
¹/₂ t. salt
2 t. poppy seed

Purée all ingredients except poppy seed in a blender until smooth; stir in poppy seed. Store in refrigerator. Makes about 1³/₄ cups.

Sandy Bernards
Valencia, CA

Christmas Tree Pull-Apart Rolls

SAUSAGE-POTATO CHOWDER

We start making this soup when the first hint of frost is in the air.

2 T. butter
1 onion, chopped
¹/₂ c. celery, sliced
3 c. potatoes, cubed
3 c. chicken broth
1 lb. smoked sausage, chopped
¹/₂ c. sour cream
10³/₄-oz. can cream of mushroom
   soup
1 c. milk

Melt butter in Dutch oven; sauté onion and celery until onion is translucent. Add potatoes and chicken broth; bring to a boil. Cover, reduce heat, add sausage and simmer until potatoes are tender, about 15 to 20 minutes. In small bowl, combine sour cream and mushroom soup; add to chowder, then stir in milk. Heat, but do not boil. Makes 6 to 8 servings.

Carol Wakefield
Indianapolis, IN

CHRISTMAS TREE PULL-APART ROLLS

Very yummy...so festive with dinner!

36 unbaked frozen rolls
2 T. butter, melted
2 t. dried parsley, crumbled
garlic salt to taste
¹/₄ c. Romano cheese, grated
additional dried parsley

Arrange rolls on a baking sheet in a Christmas tree pattern. (As they rise, the "balls" come together.) Bake according to instructions. When you remove them from the oven, they will be formed into a single piece. Transfer to a platter. Combine butter, parsley and garlic salt; brush onto rolls. Sprinkle with cheese and dried parsley. Serve immediately.

Festive garnish for meat or vegetable dishes: Use mini cookie cutters to cut shapes from potato slices; sauté until golden.

RISOTTO WITH COLLARD GREENS

This is one side dish I absolutely love!

1 onion, finely chopped
1 carrot, diced
2 T. olive oil
1 c. Arborio rice, uncooked
½ lb. fresh collard greens,
    trimmed and torn
3 cloves garlic, minced
2 14½-oz. cans chicken broth,
    heated to boiling
1 c. grated Parmesan cheese
½ t. salt
½ t. pepper

Sauté onion and carrot in olive oil in a large saucepan. Add rice and sauté until golden brown. Add collards and garlic; sauté until collards are limp. Gradually, stir in hot chicken broth. Cook, covered, on low heat until most of the liquid is absorbed, stirring occasionally. Add cheese, salt and pepper, blending well before serving.

Teresa Hill
Rochester, NY

MASHED POTATO SOUFFLÉ

Dress up your mashed potatoes for Christmas.

10 to 12 potatoes, boiled, mashed
    and seasoned with salt,
    pepper and milk
3 T. Parmesan cheese
4 eggs, beaten
2 t. onion, chopped
16-oz. pkg. shredded mozzarella
    cheese
buttered bread crumbs
parsley

After potatoes are cooked and mashed, add Parmesan cheese, eggs and onion. Spray a 13"x9"x3" baking pan with non-stick vegetable spray, then layer potatoes and mozzarella cheese in pan. Top with buttered bread crumbs and parsley. Bake at 375 for 45 to 50 minutes.

Deborah L. Crosby
Cinnaminson, NJ

Mom's Company Gelatin

mother knows best!

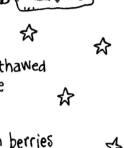

a recipe from Susan Kennedy • Delaware, Oh

2 3-oz. pkgs. raspberry gelatin
2 c. boiling water
16-oz. pkg. frozen strawberries, thawed
1-½ to 1-¾ c. crushed pineapple
1 pt. sour cream

Dissolve gelatin in water. Stir in berries & pineapple. Spread half of the mixture in a 13"x9" glass pan, reserving other half. Refrigerate mixture in glass pan 'til partially set. Spread sour cream over berry mixture. Pour remaining gelatin over sour cream. Chill until firm. Serves 14 to 16.

BROCCOLI-CHEDDAR CASSEROLE

A side dish that everyone can agree on!

8 c. broccoli, chopped
1 c. onion, finely chopped
2 T. butter
12 eggs
2 c. whipping cream
2 c. shredded Cheddar cheese,
    divided
2 t. salt
1 t. pepper

In a skillet over medium heat, sauté broccoli and onion in butter for about 5 minutes or until crisp-tender; set aside. In a large bowl, beat eggs. Add whipping cream and 1¾ cups cheese; mix well. Stir in the broccoli mixture, salt and pepper. Pour into a greased 3-quart casserole dish; set into a larger pan filled with one inch of hot water. Bake, uncovered, at 350 degrees for 45 to 50 minutes or until knife comes out clean. Sprinkle with remaining cheese; let stand for 10 minutes before serving. Makes 12 to 16 servings.

Caroline Talmage
LaGrange, IN

To allow more time for the hugs and memories, our family has begun serving prime rib for Christmas dinner. While it slowly cooks and the aroma wafts through the house, we're able to relax and enjoy one another's company.

— Debby Trapp
Baker City, OR

OLD-FASHIONED JAM CAKE

For neat slices, cut with an electric knife.

1 c. plus 6 T. shortening, divided
5¾ c. sugar, divided
½ c. water
½ c. applesauce
1 c. seedless blackberry jam
2 eggs
3 c. all-purpose flour
½ c. baking cocoa
1 t. baking powder
1 t. baking soda
½ t. salt
1 t. each ground cinnamon, ground
    allspice and ground nutmeg
1 c. buttermilk
1 c. raisins
1 c. chopped pecans
6 T. butter
1½ c. milk
1½ t. vanilla extract

BUTTERSCOTCH PIE

Great served with coffee or cappuccino!

1 c. brown sugar, packed
5 T. all-purpose flour
¼ t. salt
1 T. cornstarch
2 c. scalded milk, cooled
3 egg yolks
3 T. butter
1 t. vanilla extract
9-inch graham cracker pie crust
Garnish: whipped topping

Mix brown sugar, flour, salt and cornstarch in the top of a double boiler. Gradually add milk and cook until thick and smooth, stirring constantly. Cook for 15 minutes, stirring occasionally. In a mixing bowl, beat egg yolks until pale; stir a little of the hot mixture into them. Add to mixture in double boiler. Stirring constantly, cook 2 to 3 minutes. Add butter and vanilla; cool. Pour into pie crust and top with whipped topping. Makes 6 to 8 servings.

Jan Sofranko
Malta, IL

Beat 1 cup shortening until creamy; gradually beat in 2 cups sugar. Add water; beat until fluffy. Beat in applesauce and jam, then eggs, one at a time. Combine flour, cocoa, baking powder, baking soda, salt and spices; add to creamed mixture alternately with buttermilk. Stir in raisins and pecans. Pour into 3 lightly greased 9" round pans. Bake at 350 degrees for 24 minutes, until wooden pick inserted in center comes out clean. Cool in pans 10 minutes; remove from pans and cool completely on wire racks. Combine 3 cups sugar, remaining shortening, butter and milk in heavy saucepan. Bring to a boil; remove from heat. Put ¾ cup sugar in a separate saucepan over medium heat until sugar melts and is golden. Stirring rapidly, pour into icing in saucepan; bring to a boil over medium heat. Cook, stirring, until icing reaches soft ball stage (about 15 minutes). Remove from heat; stir in vanilla. Let stand 10 minutes, then beat icing with wooden spoon until thick and creamy but still hot. Ice between layers, on sides and top of cake; smooth with spatula dipped in hot water if necessary.

Old-Fashioned Jam Cake

Fabulous Feast for Just a Few

CRAB BISQUE

This warm and creamy soup is perfect when company's coming...serve extra cayenne at the table!

1 onion, chopped
1 stalk celery, chopped
1 carrot, chopped
1 tomato, chopped
1 head garlic, cloves peeled and halved
2 T. olive oil
2 T. fresh tarragon, chopped
2 T. fresh thyme, chopped
1 bay leaf
8 peppercorns
cayenne pepper to taste
1 c. dry sherry
4 c. chicken broth
1/4 c. tomato paste
1/2 c. whipping cream
3 T. cornstarch
2 T. water
3 6-oz cans crabmeat, undrained

Sauté first 6 ingredients together until onion is soft; drain and place in a 6-quart stockpot. Add next 6 ingredients; simmer, stirring occasionally, until most of the liquid is evaporated, about 5 minutes. Pour in broth; simmer, uncovered, for one hour, stirring occasionally. Pour mixture through a fine sieve into a large saucepan; discard solids. Whisk in tomato paste; simmer until reduced to 3 cups, about 10 minutes. Add cream; simmer 5 minutes. Stir cornstarch and water together in a small bowl; stir into bisque until thickened, about 2 minutes. Add crabmeat with juices; simmer 2 to 3 minutes or until meat is warmed through. Makes 4 to 6 servings.

Brad Sprague
Powell, OH

GARLIC PULL-APARTS

So easy to make! Serve warm with herb butter.

1/3 c. butter, melted
2 T. fresh parsley, chopped
2 T. onion, finely chopped
1 t. fresh garlic, finely chopped
1/4 t. salt
1 loaf frozen whole wheat or white bread dough, thawed and cut into 32 pieces

In a small bowl, combine butter, parsley, onion, garlic and salt.

Dip bread dough into butter mixture. Arrange bread dough in a greased 1 1/2-quart casserole or soufflé dish. Cover and let rise in a warm place until double in size. Heat oven to 375 degrees. Bake for 30 to 35 minutes or until golden brown. If bread begins to brown too quickly, shield with aluminum foil. Cool 10 minutes. Invert pan to remove bread. Serve warm. Serves 8.

Liz Plotnick-Snay
Gooseberry Patch

Crab Bisque, Garlic Pull-Aparts

HAM STEAK WITH CIDER GLAZE

This is a tasty, time-saving entrée!

1 to 2-lb. ham steak
1 c. apple cider
$\frac{1}{4}$ c. brown sugar, packed
$\frac{1}{4}$ c. Dijon mustard
$\frac{1}{4}$ c. honey
$\frac{1}{2}$ t. liquid smoke

Place ham steak in an ungreased 13"x9" baking pan; set aside. Mix remaining ingredients together; pour over ham steak. Bake at 350 degrees for 30 minutes, basting often. Serves 6.

Gail Prather
Bethel, MN

CHICKEN BREASTS CHABLIS

Delicious and tender…add mushrooms to the sauce, if you'd like!

$\frac{1}{4}$ c. all-purpose flour
1 t. salt
$\frac{1}{4}$ t. pepper
4 large boneless, skinless chicken breasts
5 T. butter, divided
2 T. olive oil
2 T. cornstarch
$1\frac{1}{2}$ c. milk
1 T. Dijon mustard
1 t. salt
$\frac{3}{4}$ c. Chablis or chicken broth
$\frac{1}{4}$ t. tarragon

Preheat oven to 350 degrees. Mix flour, salt and pepper; dredge chicken and sauté in 2 tablespoons of butter and olive oil until brown. Arrange in an 8x8-inch casserole dish. To make the sauce, whisk cornstarch into milk; set aside. Melt remaining 3 tablespoons butter in a saucepan; whisk in mustard. Cook until it comes to a boil (keep whisking) and add milk mixture, salt, wine and tarragon. Whisk and cook until it thickens. Cook one more minute, then pour over chicken. Cover; bake 45 minutes to one hour. Serve over hot cooked noodles, rice or mashed potatoes.

Chicken Breasts Chablis, Fruited Yams, Zesty Broccoli

FRUITED YAMS

This is a good side dish any time of year, but especially on blustery winter days!

2 yams, peeled and sliced
1 c. pineapple, chopped
1 banana, sliced
$\frac{3}{4}$ c. apple, peeled and chopped
$\frac{1}{4}$ c. raisins
$\frac{1}{3}$ c. apple juice
1 T. brown sugar, packed
1 t. lemon zest, grated
1 t. cinnamon
$\frac{1}{2}$ t. ground ginger
$\frac{1}{4}$ t. nutmeg

Heat oven to 350 degrees. Spray a 13"x9" baking pan with non-stick vegetable spray. Layer half of the yams in dish. Mix pineapple, banana, apple and raisins. Spread half of the fruit mixture over yams. Repeat with remaining yams and fruit mixture. Mix remaining ingredients. Pour evenly over yams and fruit mixture. Cover and bake 50 to 60 minutes or until yams are tender. Serves 6.

Cindy Watson
Gooseberry Patch

ZESTY BROCCOLI

A touch of horseradish makes this creamy broccoli dish even better!

2 10-oz. pkgs. frozen chopped broccoli
$10\frac{3}{4}$-oz. can cream of mushroom soup
$1\frac{1}{2}$ c. shredded Cheddar cheese
1 egg, beaten
$\frac{1}{4}$ c. milk
$\frac{1}{4}$ c. mayonnaise
1 T. prepared horseradish
2 T. butter, melted
$\frac{1}{4}$ c. cracker crumbs, crushed

Cook broccoli according to package instructions; drain. Combine soup, cheese, egg, milk and mayonnaise. Add horseradish. Stir into broccoli. Spoon into a greased 2-quart casserole dish. Combine butter and crumbs and sprinkle on top. Bake at 350 degrees for 45 minutes.

Barbara Arnold
Toledo, OH

"A merry Christmas to us all, my dears!"

— *Charles Dickens*

Mushrooms & Asparagus Sauté

BAKED CREAMED CORN
A well-loved addition to any meal!

2 eggs, beaten
1 c. milk
1 T. sugar
1 t. salt
2 T. butter
$\frac{1}{8}$ t. pepper
1 c. cream-style corn
$\frac{1}{4}$ c. shredded Cheddar cheese

In a large bowl, combine eggs, milk, sugar, salt, butter, pepper and corn. Pour into a greased 2-quart casserole dish. Sprinkle cheese over top. Bake at 350 degrees for 30 minutes. Makes 3 servings.

Donna Nowicki
Center City, MN

PEA & SHRIMP SALAD
This is my favorite recipe because my mom always made it for our celebrations.

15-oz. can green peas, drained
$6\frac{1}{2}$-oz. can tiny shrimp, rinsed
    and drained
1 stalk celery, chopped
2 or 3 T. mayonnaise
$\frac{1}{4}$ t. salt

Mix all ingredients in a small casserole dish; serve chilled.

Judy Voster
Neenah, WI

CRANBERRY RELISH
An easy make-ahead dish!

8-oz. can crushed pineapple with
    juice
$\frac{1}{2}$ lb. mini marshmallows
2 c. fresh cranberries, ground
1 c. sugar
1 c. whipping cream, whipped

Put crushed pineapple with juice over marshmallows; let stand overnight. Mix cranberries and sugar; let stand overnight. In the morning, combine mixtures and fold in whipped cream.

Linda Brody

CORNBREAD DRESSING
A snap to prepare, and it's a really tasty change from the more traditional bread stuffing.

4 c. cornbread, cubed
2 c. bread, cubed
$\frac{1}{2}$ c. green pepper, chopped
1 c. onion, chopped
$\frac{1}{2}$ c. celery, chopped
2 10-oz. cans chicken broth
2 eggs, beaten
2 T. dried sage
salt and pepper to taste

Lay cornbread and bread on parchment paper overnight to dry. When ready to prepare dressing, gently toss cornbread and bread cubes with green pepper, onion, celery, chicken broth, eggs, sage, salt and pepper; blend well. Spoon into a greased 9"x9" baking pan and bake at 350 degrees for 45 minutes. Makes 6 servings.

Helen Murray
Mount Vernon, OH

MUSHROOMS & ASPARAGUS SAUTÉ
Brings back fond memories of my Spring garden and reminds me to start checking my mailbox for next year's garden catalogs.

1 lb. asparagus spears, trimmed
water
2 c. sliced mushrooms
$\frac{1}{4}$ c. butter
2 T. Dijon mustard
$\frac{1}{2}$ t. garlic, minced
$\frac{1}{4}$ t. pepper
$\frac{1}{8}$ t. salt

Place asparagus spears in a 12-inch skillet; add enough water to cover. Bring to a boil over medium heat until crisp-tender; drain and set aside. Cook mushrooms in butter until tender. Add remaining ingredients; stir well and cook over medium heat until heated through; pour over asparagus. Serves 6.

Gail Prather
Bethel, MN

94

Zucchini and Tomato Sauté

a country friends' favorite side dish

2 T. onion, chopped
2 T. butter
4 medium zucchini, sliced
2 lg. tomatoes, peeled & chopped
2 T. red wine vinegar
1/2 t. dried basil leaves, crushed
1/4 t. salt
1/8 t. pepper
2 t. sesame seeds

I had no idea Santa was such a good cook!

In a large skillet, sauté onion in butter until tender. Add zucchini and tomatoes. Over low heat, cook 'til zucchini is tender-crisp. Add red wine vinegar and seasonings except for the sesame seeds. Cook 1-2 minutes more for flavors to blend. Place in a warm serving dish and sprinkle with sesame seeds.

BROWN SUGAR COFFEE
Substitute milk for cream, if you'd like.

1 c. hot, brewed coffee
2 T. whipping cream
2 T. dark brown sugar, packed
1/2 t. vanilla extract
1/4 t. ground allspice
Garnish: whipped cream or cinnamon sticks

Pour hot coffee into 2 cups or heat-proof glasses. To each cup, add half of the whipping cream, brown sugar, vanilla and allspice. Mix until smooth. Garnish each serving with a dollop of whipped cream or a cinnamon stick. Serve immediately. Makes 2 servings.

Jo Ann

AUNT LIBBY'S EGGNOG COOKIES
Another way to enjoy your holiday eggnog!

1/4 c. unsalted butter, softened
1/3 c. sugar
1 egg yolk
1 T. dark rum
1 T. whipping cream
3/4 c. cake flour
1/4 t. baking powder
dash salt
1/4 t. cinnamon

Cream butter and sugar in medium-sized bowl until light. Beat in egg yolk, rum and whipping cream. Stir together cake flour, baking powder, salt and cinnamon in a separate bowl. Stir into egg yolk mixture. Drop batter by heaping tablespoons onto ungreased baking sheet 2 inches apart. Bake at 350 degrees until cookies are puffed and lightly browned, about 15 minutes. Allow cookies to cool on baking sheet 5 to 10 minutes, then gently remove to wire rack to cool completely. Makes 10 cookies.

NO-BAKE PINEAPPLE PIE
This pie is so quick & easy to make…plus, you make it the night before!

14-oz. can sweetened condensed milk
1/4 c. lemon juice
1/3 c. maraschino cherries, chopped
1 t. vanilla extract
1/3 c. chopped pecans
8-oz. can crushed pineapple, drained
9-inch graham cracker pie crust
Garnish: frozen whipped topping, thawed, and whole maraschino cherries

Combine milk and lemon juice; stir until blended. Stir in next 4 ingredients; spoon into pie crust. Chill 8 hours or overnight. Top with whipped topping and whole cherries before serving. Serves 6 to 8.

No-Bake Pineapple Pie, Aunt Libby's Eggnog Cookies, Brown Sugar Coffee

95

Holiday Jingle Bell Lunch

Invite your friends to take a break and join you for a jingle-jolly luncheon! Serve yummy tea-room fare and enjoy an hour of holiday chit-chat with the girls

CLAY POTS MAKE IDEAL CANDLE HOLDERS. PAINT 'EM GOLD INSIDE FOR A GLOWING SHIMMER AS THE CANDLE BURNS DOWN.

FLOWERPOT CHEESE APPETIZERS
What clever serving dishes!

8-oz. pkg. cream cheese, softened
1 c. ricotta cheese
$\frac{1}{2}$ c. shredded Monterey Jack cheese
1 clove garlic, minced
$\frac{1}{2}$ c. fresh parsley, chopped and divided
$\frac{1}{8}$ t. salt
$\frac{1}{4}$ t. pepper
$\frac{1}{4}$ c. fresh chives, chopped

Blend cheeses, garlic, $\frac{1}{4}$ cup parsley, salt and pepper together until smooth; cover and chill at least one hour. Just before serving, line four new 3-inch flowerpots with plastic wrap and spoon cheese mixture into each, filling to the brim. Sprinkle with remaining parsley and chives. Serve with crackers. Makes about $2\frac{1}{2}$ cups.

Michelle Campen
Peoria, IL

For quick & easy favors, fill painted pots with mints or scented votives.

Flowerpot Cheese Appetizers

ARTICHOKE PASTA SALAD

Add diced, cooked chicken to this easy salad for a heartier dish!

Salad:
12 oz. bow tie pasta
6 oz. pitted ripe olives
8-oz. can artichoke hearts, chopped
8 oz. feta cheese, cubed
8 oz. mozzarella cheese, cubed

Cook pasta according to package directions. Drain, cool and combine with remaining salad ingredients.

Dressing:
1 clove garlic, chopped
¼ c. fresh basil, chopped
½ t. dried thyme
¼ c. shredded Parmesan cheese
¾ c. olive oil
¼ c. red wine vinegar
¼ c. balsamic vinegar
¼ t. salt
⅛ t. pepper

Place dressing ingredients in a blender and blend well. Gently toss salad mixture with salad dressing and chill. Serves 8 to 10.

Lori Davey
Owosso, MI

CRUNCHY SALAD WITH DILL DRESSING

Festive and colorful, we always take this salad to family dinners.

4 slices bacon, crisply cooked and crumbled
⅓ head romaine lettuce, torn into pieces (about 4 cups)
8 oz. cherry tomatoes, halved
½ cucumber, sliced
1 red onion, thinly sliced
½ fennel bulb, thinly sliced
½ c. plain yogurt
3 T. fresh dill, chopped
2 T. white wine vinegar
1 t. lemon zest, grated
¾ t. salt
¼ t. pepper

Crunchy Salad with Dill Dressing

KATE'S FAVORITE!

Granny's 5-cup Salad

You'll love it *almost* as much as you love your own granny!

1 c. PINEAPPLE CHUNKS OR TIDBITS, drained
1 c. MANDARIN ORANGE SEGMENTS, drained
1 c. FLAKE COCONUT
1 c. MINIATURE MARSHMALLOWS
1 c. SOUR CREAM

COMBINE ALL INGREDIENTS IN A BOWL ~ REFRIGERATE 'TIL SERVING.

In a serving bowl, combine bacon, lettuce, tomatoes, cucumber, onion and fennel. In a separate bowl, combine yogurt, dill, vinegar, lemon zest, salt and pepper. Pour dressing over salad; toss lightly to coat.

Betty Stout
Worthington, OH

Add festive color and flavor to your ice cubes...drop whole cranberries, grapes, lemon or orange slices into the ice cube trays before freezing.

country cottage chicken salad P·u·f·f·s

elegant sandwiches with a crunchy- sweet pecan topping~perfect for tea!

DID SOMEONE SAY PUFFS?

- ◆ 2½ c. cooked chicken, cubed
- ◆ 1 c. celery, finely chopped
- ◆ 4 small green onions, chopped
- ◆ 1 c. mayonnaise
- ◆ 2 t. Dijon mustard
- ◆ Salt & pepper to taste
- • frozen puff pastry, thawed
- ◆ caramelized pecans, chopped

In a mixing bowl, combine chicken, celery & green onion. Mix together Dijon mustard & mayonnaise. Pour over chicken mixture. Salt & pepper to taste~refrigerate.

Cut shapes from puff pastry using cookie cutters. Using a cutter of the same design, only smaller, make an incision about half way down in the center of the dough shape. Don't cut all the way through to bottom. Bake according to package instructions.

Remove center cutout from each baked shell carefully~Use top for a little lid. Fill shell with chicken salad just before serving. Garnish with caramelized pecans and top with puff pastry lid.

caramelized pecans

½ c. sugar   3/4 c. pecan halves

In a heavy saucepan, heat sugar over medium heat 'til melted (about 4 minutes.) Stir constantly to avoid burning sugar. Stir in pecans until well-coated. Remove pan from heat. Pour mixture onto wax paper, or onto a buttered plate. Cool. If stuck together, break apart. Use whole or coarsely chop for garnish.

★ TRY TO AVOID SNARFING THE WHOLE PLATEFUL OF PECANS YOURSELF BEFORE YOU CAN USE THEM IN THE CHICKEN SALAD... THEY ARE GOOOOOD!

Time-Saver: Use pre-cut puff pastry shells...they're available in your grocer's freezer.

Country Cottage Chicken Salad Puffs with Caramelized Pecans

98

Almond Tea Cakes, Vanilla Coffee

MOLDED CHOCOLATE CUPS

What a fun way to serve dessert...fill them any way you like!

1 c. semi-sweet chocolate chips
8 paper cupcake liners
Filling: pudding, ice cream, melted
    chocolate and peanuts,
    chocolate mousse or whipped
    cream with crushed cookies
    or candies

Partially melt the chocolate in top of double boiler over simmering water. When chocolate is partially melted, remove from heat and let it stand to melt completely. Dip a small brush into the chocolate and paint the inside of the cupcake liners, building up the sides thickly so the cups won't break when paper is removed. Turn onto a baking sheet and refrigerate until hardened. Carefully peel off the paper. Store cups in a cool area. Fill cups with favorite filling.

ALMOND TEA CAKES

When you want to serve a sweet little something.

1 c. butter, softened
1^1/$_4$ c. sugar
3 eggs
2 c. all-purpose flour
1 t. baking powder
1 t. salt
4 t. vanilla extract
^{1}/$_2$ t. almond extract
2 15-oz. pkgs slivered almonds

Cream butter and sugar with an electric mixer. Add eggs and mix well; then mix in remaining ingredients by hand. Bake in mini-muffin pans at 375 degrees 11 to 13 minutes or until done. Makes 6 dozen.

Jingle bell placemats are "sew" simple! Just use a needle and thread to attach jingle bells along the short edges of the mats, spacing them about a half-inch apart.

VANILLA COFFEE

A rich, mellow drink to enjoy with friends.

1^1/$_2$ c. milk
1 T. sugar
^{1}/$_2$ t. ground cinnamon
3 c. hot, strong brewed coffee
1^1/$_2$ t. pure vanilla extract
Garnish: frozen whipped topping,
    thawed, and ground cinnamon

Combine milk, sugar and cinnamon in a saucepan and stir well. Cook over medium heat 2 minutes, or until sugar dissolves. Remove from heat; stir in coffee and vanilla. Pour into mugs and garnish with whipped topping. Sprinkle with cinnamon. Serves 4.

Blessed are they who have the gift of making friends, for it is one of God's best gifts. —THOMAS HUGHES

Hosting a Christmas open house? Check out this selection of finger-friendly appetizers, sweets, and beverages…perfect for your guests to enjoy while they're mingling!

Artichoke-Parmesan Squares, Apricot Wraps

ARTICHOKE-PARMESAN SQUARES

Filled with so many tasty ingredients, this is sure to be a hit when you serve it to family & friends.

1¹/₂-oz. pkg. dry vegetable soup mix, divided
¹/₂ c. mayonnaise
¹/₂ c. sour cream
2 8-oz. pkgs. refrigerated crescent roll dough
10-oz. pkg. frozen chopped spinach, thawed and drained
14-oz. can artichoke hearts, drained and chopped
8-oz. can water chestnuts, drained and chopped
4 oz. feta cheese, crumbled
2 to 3 cloves garlic, pressed
¹/₂ c. pine nuts, toasted and chopped
¹/₄ c. grated Parmesan cheese

Blend together half the dry soup mix, mayonnaise and sour cream; set aside. (Use remaining soup mix for another recipe.) Unroll packages of crescent dough on a greased 15"x10" jelly-roll pan. Seal perforations of dough and press dough up sides of pan to form a crust. Bake at 375 degrees for 10 to 12 minutes or until golden. Add spinach, artichokes and water chestnuts to mayonnaise mixture; stir in feta cheese and garlic. Fold in pine nuts and spread mixture over crust. Sprinkle with Parmesan cheese. Bake an additional 10 to 12 minutes or until heated through. Cut into 2-inch squares. Makes about 35 squares.

Mary Webb
Montgomery, AL

APRICOT WRAPS

A favorite appetizer for our family no matter what the occasion…crunchy, sweet and so yummy!

14-oz. pkg. dried apricots
³/₄ c. whole almonds
1 lb. bacon
¹/₃ c. plum jelly
2 T. soy sauce
1 t. ground ginger

Wrap each apricot around an almond. Cut bacon strips into thirds widthwise; wrap a strip around each apricot and secure with a toothpick. Place on 2 ungreased 15"x10" jelly-roll pans; bake at 375 degrees for 20 minutes, turning once. In a small saucepan, combine jelly, soy sauce and ginger; cook over low heat for 5 minutes or until warm and smooth. Drain apricots on paper towels, then arrange on serving platter; serve with sauce for dipping. Makes 40 wraps.

Claire Bertram
Lexington, KY

GINGERBREAD WREATH

Set your punch bowl in the middle of this fragrant gingerbread wreath...snack on any "extra" cookies!

1 c. shortening
2½ c. brown sugar, packed
3 eggs, beaten
1½ c. molasses
6½ c. all-purpose flour
1½ T. ground ginger
2¼ t. salt
1 t. cinnamon
Optional: powdered sugar

Cream together shortening and brown sugar; add eggs and molasses. Sift together dry ingredients and add to egg mixture. Roll out dough to ¼-inch thickness on a floured surface; cut dough using 2" to 3" leaf cookie cutters. You can also use a knife to make veins in the leaves. On an ungreased baking sheet, overlap cookies into a wreath shape, leaving an opening wide enough for the base of your punch bowl and using water to "glue" the cookies onto one another. (You may not use all of the cookies.) Bake at 350 degrees for 16 to 18 minutes or until cookies are crisp and golden. Cool completely on baking sheet; let set out until hardened (this may take a day or 2). If you'd like a snowy look, handle the wreath carefully and stand it at an angle over wax paper; then dust it with powdered sugar.

Cassandra Skaggs
Valencia, CA

Gingerbread Wreath, Apple-Cinnamon Punch

CRAB DIP

Passed on to me from a friend at school, this dip is so simple!

2 8-oz. pkgs. cream cheese, softened
1 c. sour cream
1½-oz. pkg. dry vegetable soup mix
12-oz. bottle cocktail sauce
6-oz. can crabmeat, drained

Beat cream cheese until fluffy; mix in sour cream and soup mix. Mound on a small serving platter; pour cocktail sauce on top. Sprinkle with crabmeat; cover and chill for at least one hour before serving. Makes about 3 cups.

Susan Biffignani
Fenton, MO

APPLE-CINNAMON PUNCH

Make this punch for everyone to enjoy...it has a great spicy taste!

1 c. water
½ c. sugar
½ c. red cinnamon candies
2 2-ltr. bottles raspberry ginger ale, chilled
46-oz. can apple juice, chilled

Combine water, sugar and candies in a small saucepan; bring to a boil. Reduce heat and simmer, uncovered, for 5 minutes or until candies melt; stir occasionally. When mixture has cooled, combine with ginger ale and apple juice; stir well. Makes 26 cups.

Kathy Grashoff
Fort Wayne, IN

*F*loat whole cranberries and pineapple slices in your bowl of wassail.

RANCH SNACK MIX

A crunchy treat for your bunch who loves to munch.

1 envelope ranch-style dressing
　　mix
1 c. canola oil
1 t. dill weed
1 t. garlic powder
2 c. mini shredded wheat squares
2 c. mini pretzels
1 c. blanched peanuts or mixed
　　nuts
1 c. shelled sunflower seeds

Combine dressing mix, oil and seasonings; mix well. Mix remaining ingredients in a large bowl; pour oil mixture over all and stir to coat well. Spread on a baking pan and place in a 250-degree oven for 15 to 20 minutes. Stir once during baking. Store in airtight containers. Makes 6 cups.

ROASTED RED PEPPER SALSA

Fry up some quartered corn tortillas for your own fresh chips.

2 c. corn
2 tomatoes, diced
7-oz. jar roasted red peppers,
　　drained and chopped
2 green onions, finely chopped
1 jalapeño pepper, seeded and
　　minced
3 T. fresh cilantro, minced
2 T. lime juice
1 T. white vinegar
$1/2$ t. salt
$1/4$ t. pepper
$1/4$ t. cumin
2 avocados, pitted, peeled and
　　chopped

Gently stir all the ingredients together; cover and refrigerate at least 2 hours before serving. Makes $2^{1}/_{2}$ cups.

Shawna Lloyd
Flint, TX

GARLIC-FETA CHEESE SPREAD

This is a real winner!

1 clove garlic, minced
$1/4$ t. salt
$1/2$ lb. feta cheese, crumbled
$1/2$ c. mayonnaise
$1/4$ t. dried marjoram
$1/4$ t. dried dill weed, crumbled
$1/4$ t. dried basil, crumbled
$1/4$ t. dried thyme, crumbled
$3/4$ lb. cream cheese, softened

Using a fork, mash garlic into a paste; add salt. Using a food processor, blend together feta cheese, mayonnaise, garlic, herbs and cream cheese. Spoon into a crock and chill, covered, for 2 hours. Makes $1^{1}/_{2}$ cups. Serve with crackers, bagel chips or slices of pita bread.

Elizabeth McKay
Romeoville, IL

SHRIMP PUFFS

My daughter always asks me for these when she's having guests. Of course, I have to double the recipe!

$1/4$ c. grated Parmesan cheese
$1/4$ c. mayonnaise
2 T. green onion, minced
$1/4$ t. garlic powder
$2^{1}/_{2}$-oz. can cocktail shrimp,
　　drained
5 slices white bread

In a small mixing bowl, mix cheese, mayonnaise, onion and garlic powder together until blended; stir in shrimp. Cut ten 2-inch rounds from bread slices. Mound one tablespoon of the shrimp mixture onto each bread round. Place on an ungreased baking sheet. Bake at 375 degrees for 10 to 12 minutes or until golden brown. Makes 10 puffs.

Tori Willis
Champaign, IL

Roasted Red Pepper Salsa

FABULOUS FRENCH BREAD

Try slices dipped in warm marinara sauce...delicious!

1 loaf French bread
1/2 c. butter, softened
2 1/4-oz. can sliced black olives
one bunch green onions, chopped
1/4 t. garlic powder
1 c. mayonnaise
2 hot peppers, chopped
1 c. shredded Cheddar cheese

Slice bread in half lengthwise; place, cut sides up, on an ungreased baking sheet. Combine the remaining ingredients; spread over bread halves. Bake at 350 degrees for 5 to 6 minutes or until the cheese melts. Slice and serve while warm. Makes 12 servings.

Diana Krol
Nickerson, KS

CREAMY BLUE CHEESE DIP

The blue cheese makes this a tasty dip for fresh veggies or spread on warm slices of toasted French bread.

3/4 c. sour cream
1/2 t. dry mustard
1/2 t. pepper
1/4 t. garlic powder
1/8 t. salt
1 t. Worcestershire sauce
1 1/3 c. mayonnaise
4-oz. pkg. crumbled blue cheese

In a medium mixing bowl, combine sour cream, mustard, pepper, garlic powder, salt and Worcestershire sauce; blend on low speed for 2 minutes. Add mayonnaise and blend on low for 30 seconds; increase to medium speed and blend an additional 2 minutes. Slowly add blue cheese; blend on low speed for no longer than 4 more minutes. Refrigerate for 24 hours before serving. Makes 2 1/2 cups.

Teresa Sullivan
Westerville, OH

SAVORY GARLIC ALMONDS

So quick, so easy...so tasty!

1 T. butter
2 T. soy sauce
2 t. hot pepper sauce
3 cloves garlic, pressed
1 lb. blanched whole almonds
3 t. pepper
1 T. seasoned salt
1/4 t. red pepper flakes

Coat a jelly-roll pan with butter; set aside. Combine soy sauce, hot pepper sauce and garlic in a mixing bowl; add almonds, stirring until well coated. Pour mixture in a single layer into jelly-roll pan. Bake at 350 degrees for 10 minutes. Sprinkle almonds with remaining ingredients; stir. Bake for 15 minutes; cool in pan. Store in an airtight container. Makes about one pound.

COME & GET 'EM MEATBALLS

Easy to put in the oven before we leave the house...when we return, they're ready!

2 lbs. ground beef
1 1/2-oz. pkg. dry onion soup mix
1 c. bread crumbs
3 eggs, beaten
1 T. dry mustard
16-oz. can cranberry sauce
12-oz. bottle chili sauce
14-oz. can sauerkraut, drained
    and rinsed
1 1/2 c. water
2/3 c. brown sugar, packed

Mix first 5 ingredients together; shape into walnut-size balls. Arrange in an ungreased 13"x9" baking pan; set aside. Combine remaining ingredients in a saucepan; simmer for 10 minutes. Pour over meatballs; cover tightly with aluminum foil. Bake at 350 degrees for 2 hours. Serves 6.

Tori Current
Veedersburg, IN

Perfect Pickups ...No Recipes Needed!

* Use cookie cutters for cutting out finger sandwiches. Mix cream cheese with fresh herbs, spread between two pieces of cocktail bread — cut out bells, stars or gingerbread boys just for fun.

* A fresh veggie tray is always a hit! Pick up bags of pre-cut vegetables from the grocery store, along with your favorite dip. For a whimsical touch, use mini cookie cutters to cut cucumber slices, zucchini & sweet peppers into festive shapes; use little pretzel sticks to spear cheese cubes.

* Pick up grissini (crisp, skinny breadsticks) from the bakery; drop by the deli to buy a pot of herbed cheese for dipping.

* While you're at the deli, pick up a variety of Mediterranean olives for sampling!

Almond Toffee Popcorn, Best-Ever Turtles, Divinity

DIVINITY

Our family loved making divinity every Christmas. I feel so blessed to have such fond memories of the holidays and I hope, with Mom's help, to carry on the family tradition for years to come.

2 egg whites, stiffly beaten
1 t. vanilla extract
3 c. sugar
1 c. corn syrup
1 c. water
Optional: 2 drops food coloring
Optional: $^1/_4$ c. chopped walnuts

Blend egg whites and vanilla; set aside. Combine sugar, corn syrup and water in a saucepan. Stir to dissolve sugar, then bring to a boil. Continue to boil until mixture reaches the hard-ball stage or 260 degrees on a candy thermometer. Remove from heat and pour in a thin stream over egg whites. Continue to beat until mixture stands in peaks; add food coloring, if desired. Beat with a wooden spoon until candy is dull in color and holds its shape when dropped onto wax paper. Working very quickly, drop candy onto wax paper by tablespoonfuls and top with nuts, if desired. Makes 2 pounds.

Tina Kutchman
Johnstown, PA

KEY LIME BITES

The taste of that oh-so-refreshing pie in a cookie!

$^3/_4$ c. butter, softened
1 c. powdered sugar, divided
2 T. lime juice
zest of 2 limes
1 T. vanilla extract
$1^3/_4$ c. plus 2 T. all-purpose flour
2 T. cornstarch
$^1/_2$ t. salt

Cream butter and $^1/_3$ cup powdered sugar. Blend in lime juice, zest and vanilla; set aside. In a separate bowl, whisk together flour, cornstarch and salt; add to butter mixture, stirring until combined. Roll dough into a log; chill for one hour. Slice log into $^1/_8$-inch-thick rounds; place on parchment-lined baking sheets. Bake at 350 degrees for 11 to 14 minutes or until slightly golden. Place remaining powdered sugar in a large plastic bag. Remove cookies from oven and allow to cool for several minutes. While still warm, place cookies in bag with powdered sugar; toss gently to coat. Makes 2 dozen.

BEST-EVER TURTLES

We're so anxious to eat these that we set the pans of hot caramel outside to cool!

$2^1/_2$ c. pecan halves, toasted
1 c. sugar
$^3/_4$ c. corn syrup
1 c. whipping cream, divided
4 T. butter
$1^1/_2$ c. semi-sweet chocolate chips, melted

On a baking sheet, arrange pecans in sets of 3, laying 2 end-to-end and one across the top; set aside. Combine sugar, corn syrup and $^1/_2$ cup whipping cream in a heavy saucepan over medium-high heat, stirring constantly until mixture reaches a full boil. Slowly add remaining cream and butter; heat, stirring, until mixture reaches soft-ball stage or 236 degrees on a candy thermometer. Remove from heat; stir until caramel is creamy (about 5 minutes). Spoon about 1 tablespoon caramel over each set of pecans; cool. Spoon 1 teaspoon chocolate over each; let stand to harden. Makes 3 dozen.

Michele Cutler
Sandy, UT

Place a pillar candle in a clear glass container; fill halfway with fresh cranberries and tuck in holly and greens...so simple!

BROWN SUGAR PUDDIN' PIES

Bite-size brown sugar pies...great for any get-together.

15-ct. pkg. mini phyllo dough
    shells, unbaked
1/2 c. butter, softened
3/4 c. sugar
3/4 c. brown sugar, packed
2 eggs
1/2 c. half-and-half
1/2 t. vanilla extract
Garnish: nutmeg and whipped
    topping

Bake mini shells at 350 degrees for 4 to 5 minutes; set aside. Cream butter and sugars together until light and fluffy; blend in eggs, half-and-half and vanilla. Spoon into crusts; sprinkle tops with nutmeg. Bake at 350 degrees for 15 to 20 minutes or until set. Top with a dollop of whipped topping and a dusting of nutmeg before serving. Makes 15 servings.

Angela Nichols
Mt. Airy, NC

NUTTY CINNAMON CRISPS

Settle in with your favorite holiday movie and enjoy these crunchy bars.

1 c. sugar
1 c. butter, softened
1 egg, separated
2 c. all-purpose flour
1/2 t. cinnamon
1 T. water
1/2 c. chopped nuts

Beat sugar, butter and egg yolk together; stir in flour and cinnamon. Press mixture into a lightly greased 15"x10" jelly-roll pan. In a medium mixing bowl, beat egg white and water with fork until foamy; brush over dough. Sprinkle with nuts, then bake dough at 350 degrees for 20 to 25 minutes or until golden. Cut into strips and cool on wire rack. Makes 3 dozen.

Marsha Thomas
Huron, SD

Gather your friends together and serve Smooth-as-Silk Fruit Dip (But save some for yourself!)

8-oz. pkg. fat-free cream cheese, softened
1/2 c. non-fat sour cream
6 T. sugar
4 T. skim milk
1/4 t. almond extract

··· ★ ···

With an electric mixer, beat cream cheese until smooth. Blend in sour cream. Add sugar, milk & almond extract. Mix until well-blended. Refrigerate ~ serve with assorted fresh fruits for dipping.

Lowfat & Yummy!

4-CHIP MARSHMALLOW FUDGE

A fudge recipe like no other!

3/4 c. butter
14-oz. can sweetened condensed
    milk
3 T. milk
12-oz. pkg. semi-sweet chocolate
    chips
10-oz pkg. peanut butter chips
12-oz. pkg. milk chocolate chips
1 c. butterscotch chips
7-oz. jar marshmallow crème
1 1/2 t. vanilla extract
1/2 t. almond extract

Melt butter in a Dutch oven over low heat; stir in condensed milk and milk. Add chips; stir constantly until melted and smooth. Remove from heat; mix in marshmallow crème and extracts. Pour into a wax paper-lined 15"x10" baking pan; refrigerate until firm. Remove from pan; cut into squares. Makes 3 dozen.

Jill Moore
Sykesville, MD

ALMOND TOFFEE POPCORN

Crunchy and sweet...irresistible for munching on.

12 c. popped popcorn
1 c. sugar
1/2 c. butter
1/2 c. light corn syrup
1/4 c. water
1 c. chopped almonds, toasted
1/2 t. vanilla extract

Place popcorn in a large mixing bowl. In a large saucepan, combine next 5 ingredients. Cook over medium-high heat, stirring ocasionally, until candy thermometer reaches 280 degrees or soft-crack stage. Remove from heat; add vanilla and stir well. Pour over popcorn, stirring until coated. Makes about 12 cups.

Erin Jones
Smyer, TX

A 2 or 3-tier pie stand is ideal for serving a variety of cookies and candies. Set a plate on each tier and fill with goodies galore!

Arrange a wreath of rosemary and wired star garland around platters of goodies.

Two-Tone Icebox Cookies

Sliced & baked, shaped, rolled & cut or dropped…no matter how you make 'em, cookies just can't be beat!

TWO-TONE ICEBOX COOKIES
One dough makes a variety of cookies.

1 c. butter, softened
1 c. sugar
1 egg plus 1 egg yolk
1 t. vanilla extract
2³/₄ c. all-purpose flour
2 T. baking cocoa
1 egg white, beaten
1 c. almonds, finely chopped

In a large bowl, cream butter and sugar. Beat in egg and egg yolk, then beat in vanilla. Gradually add flour. Divide dough into 2 equal portions. Knead cocoa into one portion. Form each portion into a ball. Follow directions for shaping dough for pinwheel, checkerboard or bull's-eye cookies. Wrap dough in plastic wrap and refrigerate for at least 8 hours. Preheat oven to 350 degrees. For sliced cookies, cut into ¹/₄-inch slices. Space cookies 1 inch apart on a lightly greased baking sheet; bake for 8 to 10 minutes.

• CHECKERBOARD: Divide dough into ropes of light and dark. Working with 4 ropes at a time (2 of each color), press one light and one dark rope together; repeat. Place one pair of ropes on top of the other, alternating light and dark doughs. Press the ropes together to form a long roll, repeat with remaining dough. Follow directions above for refrigerating and baking.

• BULL'S-EYE: Press one color dough into a rectangle; wrap around a log of another color. It's fun to make half the cookies with dark dough centers, the other half with light dough centers. Follow directions above for refrigerating dough and baking.

• PINWHEEL: Layer 2 rectangles of different colored doughs together; roll up jelly-roll style, starting at long side. Follow directions above for refrigerating and baking.

• LOG: Roll dough into ¹/₂-inch-thick ropes; cut into 2-inch lengths. Dip logs into beaten egg white, then chopped almonds before baking.

Mary Murray
Gooseberry Patch

LICORICE SNAPS

I have baked these cookies for 23 years at Franklin Elementary School in Griffith, Indiana. I still have fond memories of their aroma while baking and their delicious taste.

1 c. butter
1 c. sugar
1 c. brown sugar, packed
1 egg
2½ c. all-purpose flour
1 t. baking soda
½ t. salt
½ t. ground cloves
½ t. cinnamon
1 T. anise seeds
½ c. chopped pecans

Cream butter and sugars. Add egg; beat until blended. Combine flour, baking soda, salt, cloves and cinnamon; add to creamed mixture. Stir in anise seeds and pecans. Divide dough in half and shape into two 10-inch-long rolls. Wrap in wax paper; chill. Cut into ¼-inch slices. Place on ungreased baking sheet. Bake at 375 degrees for 10 to 12 minutes.

Eleanore Erickson
Griffith, IN

BISCOTTI
OH BOY!

Sugar and Spice Biscotti

DELICIOUS "AS IS" OR ADD DRIED CRANBERRIES, CHERRIES OR RAISINS FOR ZIP!

¾ c. SUGAR
½ c. VEGETABLE OIL
2 EGGS
2 t. VANILLA
¼ t. SALT

1½ t. BAKING POWDER
2 c. ALL-PURPOSE FLOUR
½ c. WALNUTS, COARSELY CHOPPED
1 c. SUGAR
1 T. CINNAMON

COMBINE SUGAR & OIL TOGETHER IN MEDIUM BOWL. STIR IN EGGS & VANILLA 'TIL WELL-BLENDED. COMBINE DRY INGREDIENTS. GRADUALLY MIX IN DRY INGREDIENTS WITH WET MIXTURE. STIR IN WALNUTS. ON LIGHTLY-FLOURED SURFACE, FORM DOUGH INTO A 10" x 3" LOG. PLACE DOUGH LOG ON PARCHMENT-LINED BAKING SHEET, FLATTENING SLIGHTLY. COMBINE 1 CUP SUGAR WITH CINNAMON ~ SPRINKLE OVER LOG. BAKE AT 350° FOR 25 TO 30 MINUTES 'TIL CENTER IS FIRM. COOL 10 TO 15 MINUTES. CUT CROSSWISE INTO ½" SLICES. PLACE COOKIES CUT SIDE DOWN ON BAKING SHEET. BAKE AT 325° FOR 10 TO 20 MINUTES UNTIL BROWN AROUND EDGES & DRY. TURN ONCE DURING BAKING FOR EVEN BAKING.

DATE PINWHEELS

This recipe was passed down to me from my grandmother…it's a family favorite.

1⅓ c. chopped dates
½ c. sugar
½ c. water
½ c. chopped nuts
⅔ c. shortening
1⅓ c. brown sugar, packed
2 eggs, beaten
2⅔ c. all-purpose flour
½ t. salt
½ t. baking soda

Heat first 4 ingredients together in a saucepan, stirring until thickened; set aside. Cream shortening until light and fluffy; add brown sugar and eggs, mixing well. Sift flour, salt and baking soda together in a separate mixing bowl; add to creamed mixture. Roll dough into 2 rectangles, ¼-inch thick; spread with date mixture. Roll up jelly-roll style; wrap in wax paper and refrigerate overnight. Slice and place on greased baking sheets; bake at 375 degrees for 8 minutes or until golden. Makes about 5 dozen.

Elaine Klenow-Klemm
East Tawas, MI

Time saver: Make up the dough for slice-and-bake-cookies a month or so early, shape into logs, wrap and freeze…then just thaw, slice and bake for quick goodies!

Slice 'Em Up!

Gingerbread Babies

GINGERBREAD BABIES

Tuck them into a little box and leave them on someone's doorstep...surely you know someone who will give them a good home at Christmas!

¾ c. butter, softened
¾ c. brown sugar, packed
1 egg
½ c. dark molasses
2⅔ c. all-purpose flour
2 t. ground ginger
½ t. nutmeg
½ t. cinnamon
½ t. ground allspice
¼ t. salt

Preheat oven to 350 degrees. In mixing bowl, combine butter and brown sugar until fluffy. Add egg and molasses. In separate bowl, stir together dry ingredients. Gradually stir dry ingredients into butter mixture. Turn dough out onto well-floured surface; roll out to ⅛-inch thickness. Cut dough with a 2-inch cookie cutter; bake on a greased baking sheet for 9 to 10 minutes or until firm. Makes 12 dozen cookies.

Did you know...Cookies were "invented" by bakers of centuries past, who used dabs of cake batter to test their oven temperature! The word "cookie" comes from the Dutch word "koekje," meaning "little cake."

There is nothing like a plate of beautifully decorated cookies to highlight your Christmas table or to give to a special friend, and most of all, there is nothing like the cherished memory of making them with your children and grandchildren!

— Rebecca Suiter
Checotah, OK

Royal Icing

...hard-drying icing used by the professionals!

3 T. meringue powder
6 T. warm water
1 t. vanilla
4 c. powdered sugar
1/4 t. cream of tartar

Mix meringue powder with warm water~blend well. Combine with vanilla, sugar & cream of tartar in big bowl. Beat on low speed 'til sugar is moistened. Beat on high until glossy & stiff peaks form. The peaks should curve slightly. Divide among separate dishes & color with paste food coloring if desired. Will keep for 1 to 2 weeks in airtight refrigerated container. Use when icing comes to room temperature.

ANIMAL CRACKERS

Drizzle these with powdered sugar icing if you like, but they're great just as they are.

2 c. sugar
2 c. long-cooking oats, uncooked
1 t. baking soda
1/8 t. salt
1/2 c. shortening
1/2 c. hot water
1 1/2 t. vanilla extract
1 1/2 t. almond extract
2 to 2 1/2 c. all-purpose flour

Combine sugar, oats, baking soda and salt in a large mixing bowl; cut in shortening until crumbly. Add water and extracts; stir until blended. Add enough flour to form a stiff dough. On a lightly floured surface, roll dough to 1/8-inch thickness; cut into desired shapes. Bake on a greased baking sheet at 350 degrees for 8 to 10 minutes. Cool on wire racks. Makes about 4 dozen.

Lisa Watkins
Gooseberry Patch

ORANGE TEACAKE COOKIES

I grew up on these Orange Teacake Cookies. This recipe and my cookie jar are all I have of my grandma...but oh, what a legacy!

1 c. butter, softened
1 c. sugar
1 T. grated orange zest
1 T. orange juice
2 t. orange extract
2 eggs
3 c. all-purpose flour
1 t. baking powder

Cream butter and sugar. Add orange zest, orange juice and orange extract, then add the eggs, beating well. Sift together flour and baking powder; add to creamed mixture. Refrigerate dough until well chilled. Separate dough into thirds. Roll out 1/3 of dough at a time on floured pastry cloth. Roll thin, cut with cookie cutters and place on greased baking sheet. Sprinkle with sugar. Bake at 350 degrees for about 8 minutes.

Joy Torkelson

BROWN SUGAR & HONEY CUT-OUTS

Enjoy these spicy cookies with a tall glass of milk...perfect!

1 1/2 c. butter, softened
1 1/2 c. brown sugar, packed
1 c. honey
1 egg
5 3/4 c. all-purpose flour
2 t. cinnamon
1 t. baking powder
1 t. baking soda
1 t. ground ginger
1 T. orange zest

Cream butter and sugar until fluffy; blend in honey and egg. In another mixing bowl, combine remaining ingredients; add to sugar mixture. Chill 2 or more hours. Roll out dough on a lightly floured surface to 1/8-inch thick; cut into desired shapes with cookie cutters. Bake on greased baking sheets at 350 degrees for 8 to 10 minutes; frost with either Chocolate or Decorator Frosting when cool. Makes 5 dozen.

Chocolate Frosting:
2 c. semi-sweet chocolate chips, melted
2/3 c. sour cream

Combine warm chocolate with sour cream; stir until blended and smooth.

Decorator Frosting:
1 T. butter, softened
2 c. powdered sugar
1/2 t. almond extract
1 1/2 t. meringue powder
1 to 2 T. milk
paste food coloring

Blend all ingredients until smooth and creamy; divide into separate bowls and tint with color. Pipe designs using a pastry bag and decorating tips.

Candy Hannigan
Monument, CO

109

SANTA CLAUS COOKIE POPS

Put one at each place setting.

1 c. sugar
1/2 c. shortening
2 T. milk
1 egg
1 t. vanilla extract
2 c. all-purpose flour
1 t. baking powder
1/2 t. baking soda
1/2 t. salt
16 wooden ice-cream sticks
sugar

Preheat oven to 350 degrees. Cream sugar and shortening. Beat in milk, egg and vanilla. Stir in flour, baking powder, baking soda and salt. Shape dough into 1 1/4-inch balls. Place balls 2 inches apart on a baking sheet. Flatten each with the bottom of a glass dipped in sugar. Insert a stick into the side of each dough ball. Bake 8 to 10 minutes or until cookies are golden. Let cool on baking sheet 2 minutes. Remove from baking sheet and cool on a wire rack. Frost when completely cool.

Frosting:
1 1/2 c. powdered sugar
1/2 t. vanilla extract
2 to 3 T. water
1/4 c. red decorating sugar
1 c. shredded coconut
16 miniature marshmallows
32 raisins
16 red cinnamon candies

In a small bowl, mix powdered sugar and vanilla; add water, one teaspoon at a time, until spreadable. Spread frosting on one cookie at a time, then sprinkle red sugar on top 1/3 for a hat and coconut on bottom 1/3 for a beard. Press on a marshmallow for tassel of hat, raisins for eyes and a cinnamon candy for nose. Makes 16 cookies.

Vickie

FUDGE TRUFFLE COOKIES

The pride of the cookie exchange!

3 4-oz. bars sweet baking
    chocolate
2 T. butter-flavored shortening
1 t. instant coffee granules
3 eggs
1 1/4 c. sugar
1 t. vanilla extract
1 c. chopped pecans, toasted
6 T. all-purpose flour
1 t. cinnamon
1/2 t. baking powder
1/4 t. salt
pecan halves
3 T. sugar

Heat chocolate and shortening until melted. Remove from heat; add coffee. Stir until smooth; cool. Beat eggs and sugar 3 to 4 minutes. Beat in chocolate mixture and add vanilla. On low speed, beat in chopped pecans, flour, cinnamon, baking powder and salt. Spray baking sheets with non-stick vegetable spray. Place rounded teaspoonfuls 2 inches apart, decorating each cookie with a pecan half. Bake at 350 degrees for 8 to 10 minutes or until just set (do not overbake). Cool one or 2 minutes. Put on racks and sprinkle with sugar. Makes 3 to 4 dozen.

Santa Claus Cookie Pops

RASPBERRY RIPPLE BROWNIES

These moist, chewy brownies won't last long…you may want to make a double batch!

1 c. frozen raspberries, thawed, rinsed and drained
9 1-oz. sqs. white baking chocolate, chopped
3/4 c. all-purpose flour
1/2 t. salt
6 T. butter
3/4 c. sugar
3 eggs
1 t. vanilla extract
1 t. almond extract

Use the back of a spoon to press raspberries through a strainer to remove seeds. Measure 1/4 cup strained purée into a small bowl; set purée aside and save any additional for another recipe. Melt white chocolate in a double boiler, stirring until smooth; set aside to cool. Combine flour and salt in a small bowl; set aside. Cream butter and sugar together until smooth. Blend in eggs, vanilla and almond extract. Beat in melted chocolate; add flour mixture just until combined and the batter is smooth. Spread batter into a buttered 8"x8" pan; drizzle raspberry purée over top. Draw a thin metal spatula gently through purée to swirl it with batter until top is marbleized. Bake at 350 degrees for 35 minutes or until an inserted toothpick comes out with a few moist crumbs. Cool brownies in the pan on a wire rack for one hour. Cut into squares. Makes 12 to 16 brownies.

Raspberry Ripple Brownies

PIGNOLI (ITALIAN COOKIES)

This crunchy little cookie is perfect alongside a dish of spumoni ice cream or a cup of cappuccino.

1 lb. almond paste
1 1/4 c. sugar
4 egg whites
3 1/2 c. pine nuts or slivered almonds, depending on your preference

Break the almond paste into pieces and place in a mixing bowl with the sugar. Use a mixer to crumble the paste and sugar until evenly combined. In a separate bowl, beat the egg whites to soft peaks. Gradually fold the egg whites into the almond mixture. Place the nuts in a shallow bowl. Roll the dough into one-inch balls and press each ball into the nuts, gently turning to coat evenly. Place on a buttered baking sheet, spaced about one-inch apart. Bake 15 minutes in a 350-degree oven until light golden in color. Allow to cool 5 minutes on the pan before transferring to a rack. Store in an airtight container.

WOODCHUCKS

Deliciously crunchy!

2 c. walnuts (or 1 c. black walnuts and 1 c. pecans)
1 c. pitted dates
1 c. brown sugar, packed
2 eggs
3 1/2 c. shredded coconut, divided

Put walnuts and dates through coarse blade of a grinder or chop coarsely using steel blade of food processor or blender. Add brown sugar, eggs and 1 1/2 cups of coconut; mix well. Shape mixture into one-inch balls. Roll balls in remaining 2 cups coconut and place balls on well-greased baking sheet. Bake in a preheated, 375-degree oven 10 to 12 minutes or until coconut is toasted. Cookies will be soft, so remove them carefully from pans. They will firm up as they cool.

"Chill December brings the sleet, Blazing fire and Christmas treat."

— Mother Goose

Drop 'em out

CRANBERRY COOKIES
So tart, tender and crunchy.

3 c. cranberries
3 c. all-purpose flour
$1/4$ t. baking soda
1 t. baking powder
$1/2$ t. salt
$1/2$ c. butter, softened
1 c. sugar
1 c. brown sugar, packed
1 egg
$1/4$ c. milk
2 T. lemon juice
1 c. walnuts, chopped

Steam the cranberries 5 minutes and chop coarsely. Sift flour, baking soda, baking powder and salt together. Cream butter and sugars until light and fluffy, then beat in egg, milk and lemon juice. Stir in the flour mixture bit by bit. Add the cranberries and nuts. The cranberries will be soft and create a marbleized pattern in the dough. Drop by teaspoonfuls onto greased baking sheets, one inch apart. Bake at 375 degrees for 14 to 15 minutes, until firm and golden. Remove to racks to cool. Makes about 7 dozen.

BUTTERSCOTCH-APPLE-RAISIN COOKIES
A good, old-fashioned cookie.

$1^{1}/_{2}$ c. apples, cored, peeled and chopped
1 c. butterscotch chips
1 c. raisins
$1/2$ c. chopped nuts
$1^{1}/_{4}$ c. brown sugar, packed
$1/2$ c. butter, softened
2 eggs
$1/4$ c. milk
$1^{1}/_{4}$ c. all-purpose flour
$1^{1}/_{2}$ t. cinnamon
1 t. baking powder
1 t. salt
1 c. quick-cooking oats, uncooked

Place apples, butterscotch chips, raisins and nuts in a bowl; mix well. Combine brown sugar and butter until creamy. Add eggs and milk; beat until well blended. Sift together flour, cinnamon, baking powder and salt; stir into creamed mixture. Blend in the fruit/nut mixture; add oats. Drop by level tablespoonfuls 3 inches apart onto well-greased baking sheets. Bake at 400 degrees for 8 to 10 minutes.

Wendy Perrone

Lemon Cookies, Cranberry Cookies, Cherry Winks

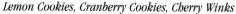

CHERRY WINKS

Make these cookies a Christmas tradition!

3/4 c. shortening
1 c. sugar
2 eggs
2 T. milk
1 t. vanilla extract
2 1/4 c. all-purpose flour
1/2 t. baking soda
1 t. baking powder
1/2 t. salt
2 1/2 c. corn flake cereal, crushed
Garnish: maraschino cherries,
    quartered

Blend together shortening, sugar, eggs, milk and vanilla; set aside. Sift together flour, baking soda, baking powder and salt; add to shortening mixture. Shape teaspoonfuls of dough into balls, roll in cereal and top each with a cherry quarter. Place cookies on a greased baking sheet and bake at 375 degrees for 10 to 12 minutes. Makes 3 dozen.

Jody Lenz
Dresser, WI

LEMON COOKIES

Very cheerful and lemony.

2 eggs
1 1/2 t. lemon extract
2 T. lemon juice
3 drops yellow food coloring
1 c. butter-flavored shortening
1/2 c. plus 2 T. lemon gelatin mix,
    divided
1 c. sugar
2 t. cream of tartar
1 t. baking soda
1/2 t. salt
2 3/4 c. all-purpose flour

Combine eggs, lemon extract, lemon juice, food coloring and shortening and beat well. In a separate bowl, combine 1/2 cup gelatin, sugar, cream of tartar, soda, salt and flour. Add to egg mixture and mix well. Drop by teaspoonfuls onto greased baking sheet. Flatten just a little with a spatula or your fingers. Sprinkle a little of remaining lemon gelatin powder over each cookie. Bake at 400 degrees just until done, about 9 minutes. Makes about 5 dozen.

Make a Wish for CHOCOLATE CHIP TWINKLES

a heavenly recipe from Marne Haag
★ Campbellsport, WI

1 c. butter, softened
3/4 c. powdered sugar
1 egg yolk, beaten
1 t. vanilla extract
1-1/4 c. all-purpose flour
3/4 c. cornstarch
1/8 t. salt
1 c. flaked coconut
1 c. semi-sweet chocolate chips
sugar

Cream butter; slowly add in powdered sugar. Blend in egg yolk & vanilla; set aside. Combine flour, cornstarch & salt; blend well into butter mixture. Stir in coconut & chocolate chips; shape into walnut-size balls and place on ungreased cookie sheets. Slightly flatten with the bottom of a glass that has been dipped in sugar; bake at 375 degrees for 12 minutes. Makes 4 dozen.

HINT HINT: For a festive Christmas cookie, place a small piece of candied cherry in the center of each cookie before baking!

Stack several home-baked cookies and wrap with ribbon or raffia...a tasty gift for a co-worker to enjoy at break-time.

Crazy ABOUT CASSEROLES

Creamy, cheesy, hearty, savory or even sweet…we simply can't resist the appeal of those heavenly casseroles! They're perfect for simple weeknight suppers, as well as carrying along to potlucks or special side dishes for holiday dinners.

Squash Casserole

SQUASH CASSEROLE
For a spicier dish, use hot sausage.

8 oz. bulk pork sausage
3 zucchini, sliced
1 onion, finely chopped
2 T. butter
2 8³/₄-oz. cans cream-style corn
2 c. shredded Monterey Jack
   cheese
³/₄ c. cornbread stuffing
4.5-oz. can chopped green chiles,
   drained

Brown sausage in a skillet, stirring until it crumbles; drain well and set aside. In a large skillet over medium heat, sauté zucchini and onion in butter until tender. Combine zucchini mixture, sausage, corn, cheese, stuffing and chiles; stir well. Spoon into a lightly greased 2-quart casserole dish. Bake uncovered at 350 degrees for 40 minutes or until golden and bubbly. Serves 8.

Joan Limberg

SEAFOOD LASAGNA

A dream come true for seafood lovers!

1/2 c. plus 2 T. butter, divided
1/2 c. all-purpose flour
4 c. milk
salt and pepper to taste
1 c. onions, chopped
3 T. olive oil
1/2 c. grated Parmesan cheese
1 lb. frozen cooked, peeled and
    deveined small shrimp, thawed
1 lb. frozen cooked bay scallops,
    thawed
2 10-oz. pkgs. fresh spinach,
    stems removed, washed and
    chopped
2 lbs. mushrooms, chopped
3 8-oz. pkgs. lasagna noodles,
    cooked
8-oz. pkg. cream cheese, cubed
2 lbs. shredded mozzarella cheese
2 lbs. crabmeat, shredded

Melt 1/2 cup butter in a large heavy pan over medium heat. Stir in flour and cook, stirring constantly; do not brown. Remove from heat and gradually whisk in milk. Return to heat and cook, whisking constantly, until thick and smooth. Season with salt and pepper; set aside. In a large skillet, sauté onions in olive oil over medium heat. Combine onions with 3 cups of prepared sauce. Stir in Parmesan cheese and fold in shrimp and scallops; set aside. Sauté mushrooms in remaining butter until tender. Add spinach and cook until wilted; set aside. Spread 1/4 cup remaining sauce in bottom of each of 2 greased 13"x9" baking pans. Layer each with 4 noodles, spread 1/4 of seafood sauce over noodles, top with 1/4 of spinach, 1/4 of cream cheese, 1/8 of mozzarella and 1/4 of crabmeat. Repeat layers, beginning and ending with noodles. Top with remaining sauce and mozzarella. Bake, uncovered, at 350 degrees for 30 minutes or until bubbly. Let stand 10 minutes before serving. Makes 12 servings.

Christi Miller
New Paris, PA

Seafood Lasagna

AUNT TILLIE'S GREEN BEANS

This recipe is one that has been a favorite in our family for years. Even though most of my family doesn't care for vegetables, they always ask for seconds of this dish!

1 lb. pkg. frozen French-style green
    beans, thawed
2 T. plus 1 t. butter, divided
2 T. all-purpose flour
1/2 t. salt
1 t. sugar
1/4 t. pepper
1/4 c. onion, finely chopped
1 c. sour cream
1/4 lb. Swiss cheese, grated
1 c. corn flake cereal, crushed

Drain beans; set aside. Melt 2 tablespoons butter over low heat; blend in flour. Stir in salt, sugar, pepper and onion. Add sour cream; stir until smooth. Remove from heat and fold in green beans. Spoon mixture into a 1 1/2-quart greased casserole dish. Sprinkle cheese over top. Layer cereal over cheese. Melt remaining butter and drizzle over cereal. Bake at 350 degrees for 30 minutes. Serves 4 to 6.

Barbara Czachowski
Dallas, TX

SPICY TEX*MEX CHICKEN

¡AY CARAMBA! COLORFUL and DELICIOUS!

6 boneless, skinless chicken breast halves
2 T. fresh lime juice
½ t. salt
¼ t. ground red pepper
⅓ c. olive oil
1 med. red onion, chopped
1 sm. red pepper, chopped
1 sm. yellow pepper, chopped
1 clove garlic, minced
¼ c. plus 2 T. fresh cilantro, chopped
6-8 ripe tomatoes, sliced
2 c. Monterey Jack cheese, shredded
cilantro sprigs for garnish
lime slices for garnish

Place chicken breast halves between wax paper ~ pound 'til slightly flat. In small bowl, combine lime juice, salt & red pepper. Add chicken to marinade ~ toss to coat. Let stand in marinade for 10-12 minutes. In large skillet, heat half of olive oil over medium heat. Sauté chicken 'til lightly browned on both sides. Remove from pan. Pour in remaining olive oil ~ heat. Sauté onions, peppers & garlic 'til tender-crisp ~ about 4-5 minutes. Remove pan from heat and add cilantro. Mix well.

Cover bottom of baking dish with ⅔s of sliced tomatoes. Layer half of onion-pepper mixture over tomato slices. Sprinkle with a bit more than just 1 cup of cheese. Place chicken on next in a single layer. Top with more tomato slices then more onion-pepper mixture. Bake for 15-25 minutes at 400° or 'til chicken is tender. Sprinkle on remaining cheese and return to oven 'til cheese is melted. Garnish with cilantro & lime slices.

Make and store casseroles ahead for quick, easy meals! Simply line a casserole dish with foil, fill with your favorite casserole, then freeze. Once the ingredients are completely frozen, lift the foil and casserole from the dish, wrap tightly in freezer wrap and return to the freezer. When you need a quick meal, pop the frozen casserole back in a dish and bake!

SCALLOPED POTATOES
Buttery, cheesy potatoes with thick slices of Kielbasa...yum!

1 c. butter
1⅓ c. all-purpose flour
6 c. milk
salt and pepper to taste
1 t. dried parsley
1 t. onion salt
1 onion, chopped
2 c. shredded Cheddar cheese, divided
½ lb. Kielbasa, sliced
10 potatoes, peeled, cubed, boiled and drained

Melt butter in a saucepan; whisk in flour until smooth. Add milk; stir until smooth and thickened. Add salt, pepper, parsley and onion salt; set aside. Pour a thin layer of sauce into a greased, 2-quart casserole dish; layer half the onion, cheese, Kielbasa and potatoes. Pour ¼ cup remaining sauce over mixture; then repeat layers, reserving ¼ cup cheese. Top with any remaining sauce and cheese. Bake one hour at 350 degrees. Serves 10 to 15.

Beth Kelly
Glassport, PA

SWEET POTATO CASSEROLE
We had this at our Christmas potluck, and it was yummy!

2½ 40-oz. cans sweet potatoes, drained and mashed
2 15.25-oz. cans pineapple chunks, drained
16-oz. can jellied cranberry sauce
10.5-oz. pkg. mini marshmallows

Layer half of sweet potatoes, pineapple, thin slices of cranberry sauce and marshmallows in a casserole dish. Repeat layers, omitting marshmallows. Bake at 350 degrees until hot in center; top with marshmallows. Once they begin to melt; broil until golden brown.

Liz Plotnick-Snay
Gooseberry Patch

CHEESY CARROT CASSEROLE

Mom was right…vegetables are good, and good for you!

2 onions, finely chopped
2 T. margarine
1/4 t. dry mustard
1/8 t. pepper
1/2 t. celery salt
1/4 c. all-purpose flour
2 c. milk
12 carrots, peeled, sliced and
    cooked
8-oz. pkg. shredded Cheddar
    cheese
1/4 c. bread crumbs

Sauté onions in margarine; stir in mustard, pepper and celery salt. Add flour and milk, stirring until combined. Stirring constantly, cook over medium heat until thickened; set aside. Layer half the carrots in a greased 1½-quart casserole dish; top with half the cheese, then half the white sauce. Repeat layers. Top with bread crumbs and bake at 350 degrees for 20 minutes or until golden and bubbly on top. Serves 6.

Linda Seidel
Reading, PA

MUSHROOM-SPINACH STRATA

If you're looking for a special recipe for a cozy dinner, this strata is easy to prepare…and so good!

1/2 c. plus 4 T. butter, divided
1/2 c. all-purpose flour
4 c. milk
1/2 c. plus 4 T. grated Parmesan
    cheese, divided
1 8-oz. pkg. sliced mushrooms
1/4 c. green onions, chopped
2 8-oz. pkgs. cream cheese,
    softened
2 eggs, beaten
3 10-oz. pkgs. frozen spinach,
    thawed and drained
8 10-inch flour tortillas

Prepare white sauce by melting 1/2 cup butter in a large saucepan over medium heat. Whisk in flour; cook one minute. Gradually add milk; cook 12 minutes, stirring constantly or until slightly thickened. Stir in 4 tablespoons Parmesan cheese; set aside. Sauté mushrooms and onions in remaining 4 tablespoons butter; add one cup of white sauce and set aside. Mix cream cheese, eggs, spinach and 1½ cups of white sauce. Grease a 15"x10" casserole dish. Spread bottom of dish with 1/2 cup of white sauce. Layer 2 tortillas on top of white sauce, then 1/2 of spinach mixture, then 2 tortillas, mushrooms, 2 tortillas, remaining spinach mixture and 2 remaining tortillas. Top with one cup of white sauce and remaining 1/2 cup of Parmesan cheese. Bake at 350 degrees for one hour. Let stand 5 minutes before serving.

Julie Dobson
Loma Linda, CA

Don't serve your special holiday recipes in ordinary, everyday casserole dishes…look for colorful stoneware or seasonal designs to showcase your culinary talents!

Mushroom-Spinach Strata

PENNE PASTA WITH TOMATOES

I love this pasta dish in the winter when practically everything is out of season and I'm bored with all my "family standards."

6 T. olive oil, divided
1¹/₂ c. onion, chopped
1 t. garlic, minced
3 28-oz. cans Italian plum
    tomatoes, drained
2 t. fresh basil, chopped
1¹/₂ t. red pepper flakes
2 c. chicken broth
salt and pepper to taste
1 lb. penne pasta
2¹/₂ c. Havarti cheese, grated
¹/₂ c. Kalamata olives, sliced
¹/₂ c. fresh Parmesan cheese,
    grated
Garnish: ¹/₄ c. fresh basil,
    chopped

Heat 3 tablespoons oil in a Dutch oven over medium-high heat. Sauté onion and garlic for 5 minutes. Add tomatoes, basil and red pepper flakes; bring to a boil. Break tomatoes with the back of a spoon, then add broth. Reduce heat and simmer one hour. Add salt and pepper; set aside. Cook pasta according to package directions; drain. Toss with remaining 3 tablespoons oil and combine with tomato sauce. Stir in Havarti cheese. Pour in a 13"x9" casserole dish. Top with olives, then Parmesan. Bake 30 minutes at 375 degrees. Sprinkle fresh basil on top before serving. Serves 6 to 8.

Dana Stewart

Penne Pasta with Tomatoes

MARY ELIZABETH'S NO-NONSENSE METHOD OF
TRANSPORTING A CASSEROLE
HOT from the OVEN

1. Wrap it immediately in foil.
2. Then wrap it in a quilted casserole cozy. (If you don't have one, several layers of newspaper will do the trick.)
3. Now wrap that in a towel and place it in a box so it won't slide around.
4. Go!

CREAMY MACARONI & CHEESE

The spicy brown mustard gives this a little kick!

6 T. butter, divided
3 T. all-purpose flour
2 c. milk
8-oz. pkg. cream cheese, cubed
2 c. shredded Cheddar cheese
2 t. spicy brown mustard
1/2 t. salt
1/4 t. pepper
8-oz. pkg. elbow macaroni, cooked
3/4 c. bread crumbs
2 T. fresh parsley, minced

Melt 4 tablespoons butter in a large saucepan. Stir in flour until smooth. Gradually add milk; bring to a boil. Cook and stir for 2 minutes. Reduce heat; add cheeses, mustard, salt and pepper. Stir until cheese is melted and sauce is smooth. Add macaroni to cheese sauce; stir to coat. Transfer to a 3-quart casserole dish. In a small saucepan, melt the remaining 2 tablespoons butter and toss with bread crumbs and parsley; sprinkle over macaroni. Bake, uncovered, at 400 degrees for 15 to 20 minutes or until golden brown. Makes 6 to 8 servings.

Liz Brady
Manchester, NH

"Animal crackers
and cocoa to drink.
That is the finest
of suppers, I think.
When I'm grown up and
can have what I please,
I think I shall always
insist upon these."

— Christopher Morley

"It is probably illegal to make
soups, stews and casseroles
without plenty of onions."

— Maggie Waldron

PORK CHOPS & STUFFING

I've been making this recipe for 28 years and it's still one of my favorites! The mandarin oranges and brown sugar make it special.

6 pork chops
1 T. shortening
2 t. salt, divided
1 c. celery, chopped
3/4 c. onion, chopped
1/4 c. butter, melted
1/4 c. brown sugar, packed
5 c. bread, cubed
1 egg, beaten
1 t. dried sage
1/2 t. dried thyme
1/8 t. pepper
11-oz. can mandarin oranges, drained

Brown pork chops in shortening; remove to a platter and season with one teaspoon salt. Lightly brown celery and onion in melted butter; stir in brown sugar. Combine bread cubes with egg, sage, thyme, pepper and remaining one teaspoon salt; add to vegetables. Stir in oranges and mix gently. Spoon stuffing into the center of a 10-inch casserole dish. Place pork chops around the stuffing and cover with foil. Bake at 325 degrees for one hour and 15 minutes. Makes 6 servings.

Barbara Schmeckpeper
Elwood, IL

For a sweet holiday surprise, invite someone who lives alone to dinner this week... you'll both enjoy the real spirit of the season.

KIDS' CHOICE PIZZA DISH

A TASTY DINNER THAT PLEASES ALL KIDS, BIG AND SMALL!

8 OZ. PKG. EXTRA WIDE NOODLES
1 LB. GROUND BEEF
4 OZ. PKG. PEPPERONI, SLICED

32 OZ. JAR PIZZA SAUCE
2 c. MOZZARELLA CHEESE, SHREDDED

COOK NOODLES ACCORDING TO PACKAGE ~ DRAIN. BROWN GROUND BEEF IN SKILLET ~ DRAIN OFF FAT. ADD SLICED PEPPERONI ~ COOK ABOUT 3 MINUTES. STIR IN PIZZA SAUCE ~ SIMMER FOR 10 MINUTES. MIX SAUCE WITH NOODLES ~ TURN INTO LIGHTLY-GREASED CASSEROLE DISH. TOP WITH SHREDDED MOZZARELLA. BAKE AT 350° UNTIL BUBBLY, ABOUT 20 MINUTES.

★ ADULT ADDITIONS MIGHT INCLUDE ONIONS, GREEN PEPPERS, SLICED CANNED MUSHROOMS & BROWNED ITALIAN SAUSAGE.

EAT it UP!

INSTRUCTIONS

FAMILY MEMORY WREATH

(shown on pages 8 and 9)
This memory-filled "charm bracelet" wreath is truly as unique as each family when filled with reminders of the important things in their lives…a flag for a loved one in the service, a carriage with a tiny doll for each new grandchild as they come along, wedding or graduation trinkets and tiny toys to represent favorite hobbies or sports.

Gather mementos and souvenirs from each family member's collection of treasures and hot glue or wire them to an artificial wreath that has been entwined with pretty ribbon. Glue wooden tile letters to a piece of wire to spell out meaningful words…if you don't have tiles, simply stamp letters, or photocopy ours from page 137, onto card stock, then cut the card stock into "tiles." Glue the words to the wreath. Your wreath may not be really full the first year, so tuck in sprigs of artificial greenery to be replaced in future years with more "charms."

FRAMED PRINTS

(shown on page 10)
Watch those precious tiny hands or feet "grow up" year after year with this seasonal "growth record."

HAND OR FOOTPRINTS

Dab the child's hand or foot with bright red paint, then lightly blot it on a paper towel; stamp the print onto a cream-colored piece of card stock that fits into an almost-white wooden frame with no easel. Add a sticker border along the frame opening. Stamp, write or paint the child's name below the print.
For the hanger, cut a piece of wide ribbon 4-times longer than the frame is tall; follow page 134 to tie a bow with a center loop at the center of the ribbon. Glue the streamers to the removable back of the frame.

BACK OF FRAME PHOTO

For the photo mat, cut a piece of cardboard ½" smaller on all sides than the frame. Cover the cardboard with Christmasy scrapbook paper. Use hook and loop dots at each corner to adhere the mat to the back of the frame.

For the photo frame, cut a piece of card stock ¼" larger on all sides than your photograph (use decorative-edge craft scissors if desired). For the photo corners, cut four 2" long lengths of ribbon. Wrapping and gluing the ends to the back, place a length of ribbon diagonally across each corner of the card stock. Stamp the year onto a piece of card stock, then cut it out. Glue the photo frame to the mat; use clear self-adhesive photo corners to attach the year to the mat.

Something extra: Glue the sides and bottom of a large Christmas envelope onto the backside of the photo mat for a pocket to hold the stamped prints and photographs as they are replaced each year.

MEMORY JOURNAL

(shown on page 11)
Christmas family gatherings spur fun trips down memory lane. Encourage everyone to write their own favorites in a memory journal…include stories, songs, recipes, antidotes or just have them add their name to show they were there that Christmas.

Stamp your family name and "Our Christmas Journal" onto craft paper. Cut out the letters and the words; glue the name along the left edge of a spiral-bound journal. Wrapping and gluing edges to the inside and starting about 1" from the letters, cover the front of the journal with seasonal-motif scrapbook paper; glue ribbon along the left edge of the paper.

Glue postcards or the front of Christmas cards onto card stock, then cut out the card stock ¼" outside the edge of the cards. Glue the cards to the journal.

To finish the journal, cut a piece of card stock just smaller than the inside front cover; glue in place to cover paper edges.

MEMORY BOX
(shown on page 12)

- acrylic primer
- wooden box with hinged lid (ours measures 15"x9¹/₂"x5")
- wooden drawer knob
- 8"x10" wooden picture frame with a flat back
- ivory and red acrylic paints
- paintbrushes
- 2¹/₂" wide foam brush
- sandpaper
- tack cloth
- ivory paint pen
- craft glue
- iridescent glitter
- clear acrylic matte spray sealer
- black & white checked self-adhesive border stickers
- corrugated cardboard
- decorative paper
- ivory card stock
- small glittery snowflake cut-outs

1. Prime the box, knob and frame, then paint them ivory. Paint the top of the lid red.

2. Use the foam brush to paint red stripes along the box and edges of the lid; add a red dot to the center of each ivory section on the box. Lightly sand the box to give it an aged look, then wipe it with a tack cloth.

3. Use the paint pen to draw a snowflake on each red section around the box and on each side of the lid; draw a line with a dot at each end above and below the snowflakes on the lid.

4. Working on one snowflake at a time; draw over each snowflake with glue, then cover glue with glitter. Allow the glue to dry, then shake off excess glitter.

5. Glue the knob to the front center edge of the lid. Apply 2 coats of sealer to the box and frame. Adhere a sticker border around the opening of the frame. Cut a piece of cardboard and decorative paper to fit in the frame.

6. Photocopy the label pattern on page 138 onto card stock; cut out. Glue the label, then the snowflake cut-outs, to the decorative paper. Secure the label and cardboard in the frame; glue the frame to the lid.

"WISHES" JOURNAL
(shown on page 13)
Have the family write (or cut and paste pictures of) their heart's desires in this little journal…it will help with shopping this year and will be fun to look back at many years from now!

Size the "wishes" pattern on page 138 to fit your spiral-bound journal; transfer the pattern to the front. Use a sage-colored paint pen to draw over the letters, then use a silver paint pen to add accent outlines and details to the letters. Use a fine-point black marker to outline part of each letter; use the silver and a gold paint pen to draw stars, snowflakes and dots around the letters. Glue iridescent glitter to the cover as desired. Allow the glue to dry, then shake off the excess glitter. Use brush-on clear acrylic matte sealer to seal the front of the journal.

Randomly adding assorted shapes of sparkly beads, loosely coil and wrap lengths of gold craft wire through and around the spiral binding. Be careful to not thread the wire too tightly or add too many beads or the journal won't open. Curly-q the ends of the wires.

MEDIA COVERS
(shown on page 13)
The perfect memories to add to your Memory Box from page 12 is a video recording of your family's holiday gatherings all decked out in a Christmasy protective covering.

VCR Sleeves
Wrap a piece of decorative card stock around the VCR tape box…make sure you crease the paper along the box edges and cut a little flap to glue the beginning and ending edges together. Tie it up with a length of ribbon, then add an ID Label (instructions follow).

Camcorder Cassette Cover
Start out the same as the VCR sleeve, except don't glue the edges together. Instead, start by matching the edge of the card stock with the edge of the lid and glue the paper to the case…trim the corners of the flap. Do the same with a length of ribbon, then add a hook and look fastener to the ribbon ends to keep it closed. Finish it off with a purchased tag embellished with the year. Use raffia and a button to attach it to the ribbon closure.

DVD Cover
Cut out a 5¹/₄"x12¹/₂" rectangle from decorative card stock. Fold the card stock at 5" and 10" from one short edge…glue the cover edges together. Attach a hook and loop fastener to the flap, then add an ID Label (instructions follow).

(continued on page 122)

LABELS

Cut a 2"x3" tag from card stock. Glue the tag to another piece of card stock and add a large sticker along the left edge. Cut out the tag and sticker. Use a fine-point marker or stamps and an inkpad to write the year and event on the tag. As a VCR label, glue the entire tag to the front of the box. As a DVD label, glue the top half of the tag to the flap…leave the bottom unglued so the flap will open.

STORY-TIME SANTA BLANKET
(shown on page 14)
- tracing paper
- fleece stadium blanket
- white, brown, blue and red embroidery thread
- red, flesh, white, blue, black and brown felt
- white fake fur
- fusible batting
- clear-drying fabric glue
- polyester fiberfill
- cosmetic blush

Use 3 strands of embroidery floss for all stitching unless otherwise indicated. Refer to Embroidery Stitches, page 135, for some "how-to" help from your Country Friends®. Refer to the Santa blanket photo for placement when assembling Santa and embellishing with embroidery stitches.

1. Hand letter 2" tall words from a favorite Christmas story on tracing paper. Pin the words along the edges of one corner of the blanket. Stitching through the paper and using 6 strands of floss, work *Backstitches* along the letters; carefully remove the paper. Work a white *Straight Stitch* snowflake in the corner.

2. Trace the patterns from pages 140 to 143 onto tracing paper. Refer to *Making Patterns, page 133,* to make an entire beard. Using the patterns, cut a hat and lips from red felt; face from flesh felt; beard, each eyebrow, white of eye and two mustaches from white felt; pupil from blue felt; mouth from black felt; winking eye and open eye background from brown felt; and hat trim and pom-pom from fur. Reversing the patterns, cut a hat and beard from batting.

3. Fuse the batting pieces to the wrong side of the hat and beard felt pieces. Stack the mustache pieces together and stitch along the bottom edge.

4. Arrange the face on the beard, then glue the top and bottom edges in place. Glue the bottom edge of the hat to the top of the face. Layer and glue the eyebrows, winking eye and open eye pieces on the face. Arrange, then glue the mouth, lips and top of mustache on the beard. Stitch down the center of the mustache.

5. Place a small amount of fiberfill between the layers of the cheeks and beard. Work several black *French Knots* for an iris, then a white snowflake *Straight Stitch* highlight on the open eye. Work brown *Straight Stitch* "crow's feet" by the winking eye and *Running Stitches* for the nose; *Backstitch* along the tops of the cheeks. Make a pink *French Knot* highlight on the lips.

6. Pin the Santa to the embellished corner of the blanket. Work white *Running Stitches* along the edge of the beard and red *Running Stitches* along the edges of the hat. Work white *Running Stitch* curls on the beard.

7. Glue the trim and pom-pom to the hat. Glue the tips of the mustache in place. Lightly highlight cheeks and nose with blush.

8. For the fur tassel on the corner of the blanket, cut a 2" square of fur, then baste along the edges; gather edges tight and tie thread to secure. Sew tassel to corner of blanket.

JINGLE LETTERS
(shown on pages 16 and 17)
Santa will stop and admire your hearth when he sees this fun arrangement of his favorite "sound!"

Prime, then paint 6" tall wooden letters that spell out "jingle." For each letter, place a piece of tracing paper on the face of the letter, then rub a crayon along the front edges to make a pattern. Use the pattern to cut decorative paper to fit the letter. Glue the paper to the letter, then embellish with self-adhesive stickers. Nestle the decorated letters into a plush garland of wintry greenery adorned with large white jingle bells tucked here and there.

BABY'S FIRST STOCKING
(shown on page 18)
Trace the stocking pattern from page 139 onto tracing paper; cut pattern out. Use the pattern to cut 2 stocking pieces (one in reverse) from white velvet and 2 lining pieces from linen. Cut a 5"x9" cuff from linen.

Matching right sides, using a 1/2" seam allowance and leaving the top open, sew velvet pieces together; turn right-side out. Leaving the top open, sew lining pieces together. Matching right sides, sew ends of cuff together. Matching wrong sides and long edges, fold cuff in half; press cuff.

Matching top edges, place lining in stocking. Matching top raw edges, and cuff seam to stocking heel seam, place cuff inside lining. Sew pieces together along the top edges. Fold cuff to the outside. For the hanger, fold a 5" length of sheer ribbon in half; tack the ends inside the cuff at the heel-side seam.

Embellish the cuff with white button and silver and white seed bead "flowers." For the name, string white and silver seed beads (length of name will determine how many beads will fit between the letter beads) and letter beads onto nylon thread; scallop and tack the string of beads along the edge of the cuff. Tack the center of a length of ribbon to the cuff with a button.

TREE PILLOW SHAM
(shown on pages 26 and 27)
- green and red velveteen
- wired red pom-pom trim
- white fur fabric
- silver jingle bells
- red chenille fringe trim
- polyester fiberfill or pillow to fit in sham

Use a 1/2" seam allowance for all sewing unless otherwise indicated.

1. Enlarge the tree pattern on page 156 by 167%. Use the pattern to cut 2 tree shapes from green velveteen. Matching right sides and leaving an opening for turning, sew the edges together; turn right-side out and stitch opening closed. Arrange and pin pom-pom trim on the front of the tree; tack in place.

2. For the sham front, cut one 13"x16" center from white fur and two 7"x16" ends from green velveteen. Matching right sides and long edges, sew one end piece to each side of the center piece; trim the seams. Arrange the tree on the center piece, then tack in place. Stitching through the tree and fur layers, sew bells on the tree.

3. Matching straight edges and overlapping trim at center bottom, baste fringe trim along the edges on the right side of the sham front.

4. For the sham back, cut two 14 1/2"x16" back pieces from red velveteen. Press one 16" edge on each back piece 1/4" to the wrong side twice; sew in place. Matching right sides and raw edges and overlapping hemmed edges at center back, pin the back pieces to the sham front; sew pieces together along outer edges. Turn the sham right-side out, then insert fiberfill or pillow.

OVERSIZED STOCKING
(shown on pages 26 and 27)
- green cotton velveteen
- white artificial fur fabric
- white lining fabric
- wired red pom-pom trim
- red chenille fringe trim
- 8" length of 1" wide red grosgrain ribbon
- 2 silver 3/4" diameter jingle bells

Use a 1/2" seam allowance for all sewing.

1. Enlarge the stocking and cuff patterns on page 145 by 167%. Draw, then cut out a 7 1/2"x8" rectangle pattern on paper. Tape the rectangle along dashed line on stocking pattern; draw an entire stocking pattern. Use the pattern to cut 2 stocking pieces (one in reverse) from velveteen and 2 liner stocking pieces (one in reverse) and one cuff liner from lining fabric. Refer to *Making Patterns*, page 133 to make an entire cuff pattern. Use the pattern to cut one cuff liner from lining fabric

2. Arrange and pin pom-pom trim along toe and heel on stocking front; tack trim in place.

3. Matching right sides, place velveteen stocking pieces together. Leaving top open, sew edges together; trim seam, then turn right-side out. Matching right sides, place liner stocking pieces together; leaving the bottom edges open for turning and the top open, sew sides together, then trim the seams.

4. Matching right sides, place cuff and cuff liner together; sew scalloped edges together. Trim seam; clip curves and open cuff. Matching right sides and short edges, fold cuff in half and sew short edges together. Matching raw edges, fold lining to wrong side of fur cuff.

5. Matching top edges and cuff seam to stocking heel seam, place cuff over stocking. Matching top edges, place cuff/stocking in liner stocking. Sew top edges together. Pull stocking and cuff out of liner; stitch opening in bottom of liner closed. Tuck liner in stocking.

(continued on page 124)

6. Tack fringe trim to stocking just above the bottom edge of the cuff...the flange on the trim will be covered by the bottom of the cuff. Fold the ribbon in half, then stitch the ends inside the stocking at the heel seam for the hanger. Sew bells to the cuff and toe of the stocking.

HEADBOARD WREATH
(shown on page 28)
For a unique garland, write the names of friends & family members on adding machine paper. Carefully wrap the list garland and some red chenille yarn around an artificial evergreen wreath...wire on a few large silver jingle bells and some red miniature ornament picks here and there.

Enlarge the ink bottle and letter patterns, page 146, to fit on your wreath. Use the patterns, to cut letters and a bottle from self-adhesive black felt. Adhere each cut-out to white felt; cut out the white felt 1/4" larger than the black cut-out. Glue a white paper "ink" label on the bottle. Arrange and glue the felt pieces, a red ribbon bow, a pair of eyeglasses and a plush white feather for the quill on the wreath.

PLACEMAT PILLOW
(shown on page 28)
Matching right sides, place 2 large rectangle-shaped fabric placemats together; sew the top and bottom edges together, then turn the tube right-side out. Follow manufacturer's instructions to cover six 1 1/2" diameter buttons with white chenille. Stuff a pillow form into the tube; sew 3 buttons across each end of tube to secure pillow form in place. Voilà! Done in the twinkle of an eye!

MENU BOARD
(shown on page 32)
Greet your breakfast guests with a message written on this cheery tabletop message board you can decorate in just a few minutes. Simply adhere border stickers along the edges of the chalkboard and across the chalk tray; glue a button at each corner of the chalkboard. Use crisp wide ribbon to tie a bow, then glue sprigs of greenery and red berries to the knot of the bow. Glue the bow to the message board.

MITTEN PLACECARD
(shown on page 33)
Cut a 2 1/4"x3 1/2" piece of green card stock, a 1 1/2"x3" piece of cream card stock and tear a 2"x3 1/4" piece from red handmade paper...use a craft glue stick to glue the pieces together for the tag. Attach a 1/4" diameter grommet through each corner of the cream part of the tag. Gluing the ends to the back and leaving 1" tails at the upper right corner, thread 1/8" wide ribbon through the grommets to make a frame. Write, draw or stamp the name on the tag. Hot glue a sprig of greenery and a button to the top right corner, then tack or glue the tag to a purchased mitten.

DECORATED CAKE STAND
(shown on page 34)
For the sparkly spots on the stand, cut 1" diameter circles from double-sided adhesive sheets. Adhere the spots to the cake cover, then cover them with iridescent glitter. Wire a wintry mix of greenery and red berries together, then add a big plaid bow and wire the arrangement to the top of the cover...quick & easy to make and versatile enough to leave out all year 'round.

CASSEROLE COZY
(shown on page 35)
• tape
• 1/2 yard of fabric
• 1/2 yard of low-loft batting
• buttons
• 1/2 yard of 3/8" wide grosgrain ribbon

This cozy fits a 9"x13" glass baking dish with handles.

1. Enlarge the cozy pattern on page 147 by 167%, then make 3 more copies of it. Cut out each pattern piece, then tape them together to make an entire pattern. Use the pattern to cut 2 pieces each from fabric and batting.

2. Matching right sides and raw edges, place fabric pieces together; stack batting pieces on top of the fabric pieces. Using a 1/2" seam allowance and leaving an opening for turning, sew pieces together. Turn right side out and sew opening closed.

3. Tack top corners together at each corner of cozy; sew a button at each corner.

4. For each handle, fold the handle part of the cozy in half and tack at the inner corners to secure. Sew a folded length of ribbon and a button over each tacked corner.

PHOTO ORNAMENTS
(shown on page 39)
Ever wonder what to do with all of those small photographs? These tiny "picture frames" are a wonderful way to preserve the photograph AND display them at Christmastime with your other favorites.

For each frame, trim the width of the photo to match the width of a clear microscope slide. Cut 2 pieces of glass the same length of the photograph…to cut the glass, use a glass cutter and ruler to score the glass at the necessary length. Place the glass (scored line up) on a pencil on a flat surface and gently push the ends down…be sure to wear safety goggles…the glass will snap into 2 pieces.

Sandwich the photo between the 2 pieces of glass. Wrapping edges to the front and back and mitering the corners, cover the edges with $1/4$" wide self-adhesive silvered copper foil. Leaving the eye extending above the frame (and another one below the frame if you want to connect more than one frame together), glue a silver eye pin to the back of the frame. Draw around the frame on black self-adhesive felt, then cut the felt out and adhere it to the back of the frame. Attach a $1/2$" diameter jump ring to the eye pin, add a ribbon hanger and you're ready to start on the next frame!

STUFFED TEDDY BEAR
(continued from page 43)

6. Matching double triangles, sew the body back pieces together; matching triple triangles, sew the body front pieces together. Matching single triangles, sew the front and back pieces together (this is the sides of the bear). Trim fur $1/4$" from the neck edge; baste, then gather the top of the body opening tightly and tie threads to secure gathers. Turn body right-side out.

7. For each joint, place a washer, then one hardboard piece onto a cotter pin. Place one joint piece inside each arm and leg. Working from the inside out, push the cotter pin piece through the fabric at the joint placement mark. Place remaining joint piece inside the head; push the cotter pin from inside the head out through the gathers in the neck.

8. Assembling one at a time and making sure you place the left and right arms and legs on the correct side of the body, push the leg and arm cotter pins (from inside out) through the joint placement marks inside the body. Place another hardboard disc, then washer onto the cotter pin. Push discs tight together, then spread the prongs on the cotter pin to secure them in place. For the head, push the cotter pin in the head through the gathers in the body. Place the remaining hardboard disc, then washer onto the pin; push discs to tighten, then spread the pin prongs.

9. Firmly stuff legs, arms, head and body and sew openings closed. Use a small knitting needle to pull fur out of the seams to cover the seams.

10. Trim fur on the face to about $1/8$" long to shape a muzzle area around the nose and mouth.

11. Using 6 strands of floss, work a triangle-shaped *Satin Stitch* (page 135) nose on the face; work *Backstitch* "claws" on the feet and paws and under the nose for a mouth.

DOOR TAGS
(shown on page 46)
• three 18"x24" pieces of white corrugated plastic
• blue and black acrylic paint
• 1" wide foam brush
• transfer paper
• craft glue
• iridescent glitter
• large clear iridescent sequins
• several **Wooden Snowflakes**, page 49
• $2^1/2$" wide wire-edged ribbon
• 3M™ Command™ Adhesive strips

1. For the tags, trim 2 corners from one end of each plastic piece. Cut a hole in the end for the ribbon.

2. Paint a 1" wide blue border around the edges of each tag. Enlarge the "Let It Snow" patterns, page 154, 200%. Transfer one word to each tag. Paint the words black.

3. For each tag, apply a thin layer of glue to the words and border, then sprinkle the glued areas with glitter; glue sequins randomly to the tags. When glue is dry, gently remove excess glitter.

4. Glue several **Wooden Snowflakes** to each tag and tie a length of ribbon through each hole. Use the self-adhesive strips to attach the tags to your front door.

BEADED STAR TREE TOPPER

(shown on page 51)

Alternating colors and curling wire around a pencil 2 or 3 times before and after adding 6 or 7 beads, thread 20mm red and 11x12mm natural wooden beads onto about 48" of gold 14-gauge wire (if wire needs pieced, just twist ends together - the beads will cover it) to make one segment; make 10 segments. When you are through adding beads, twist the wire ends together, then trim them. Bending wire between segments, form a star shape; use craft wire to secure the star in the top of the tree.

FRINGED GARLAND

(shown on page 51)

How much garland you make will depend on how large your tree is…just keep sewing sections together until you have enough to trim your tree.

For each garland section, cut a 5" wide strip from red fleece. Fold the strip in half lengthwise and sew ¼" from the fold. Cutting to within ½" of fold and at ½" intervals, make clips along the long edge for fringe.

ARGYLE AND HEART FELT ORNAMENTS

(shown on page 52)

ARGYLE ORNAMENT

Cut one 4-block square from argyle-patterned fleece. Using 6 strands of embroidery floss and stitching along the square's edges, sew the square to a piece of fur fleece…before you finish sewing the square on, lightly stuff the ornament with polyester fiberfill. Use pinking sheers to trim the fur fleece to ¼" larger than the square. Sew a wooden button to the center of the ornament.

For the tassel, cut a 2"x6" piece from red fleece. Cutting to within ½" of opposite long edge and at ½" intervals, make clips along the strip for fringe. Roll the uncut long edge into a tight roll…sew together along the top coil. Sew end in place. Insert the needle up through the center of the tassel, then through a wooden bead. Sew the tassel to one corner of the ornament. Thread a 6" length of floss through the ornament corner opposite the tassel; tie the ends together for a hanger.

HEART ORNAMENT

Trace the heart pattern on page 141 onto tracing paper. Use the pattern to cut a heart from red fleece. Using 6 strands of embroidery floss and stitching along the heart's edges, sew the heart to a piece of fur fleece…before you finish sewing the heart on, lightly stuff the ornament with polyester fiberfill. Trim the fur fleece to ¼" larger than the heart. Sew a wooden button to the center of the ornament.

For the tassel, knot a length of floss at the bottom of the ornament. Making several knots above and below each button to hold buttons in place, thread 3 buttons onto the floss. Thread a 6" length of floss through the top center of the ornament; tie the ends together for a hanger.

BEADED CANDY CANES

(shown on page 52)

For each candy cane, alternating colors, thread 20mm red and 11x12mm natural wooden beads onto a 12" piece of 14-gauge green wire. Curl each wire end to hold the beads in place. Shape the beaded wire into a candy cane shape. Attach a red heart charm to the top curl.

PIECED TREE SKIRT

(shown on page 52)

1. This is an easy skirt to make, but first you'll have to make a pattern. You will need an 18"x36" piece of paper…use wrapping or kraft paper or just tape sheets of printer paper together.

2. Referring to Fig. 1, mark points **A** and **B** 1" from the left edge of the paper. Mark point **C** 16" from point **B**, then draw straight lines from point **A** to points **B** and **C**. Working from point **A**, use a compass set to 2" to make a curved line between the lines; draw a dotted cutting line 1½" from point **A**. Draw a dotted cutting line ½" from the **AC** line.

Fig. 1

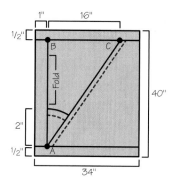

3. Next, you are going to need a really big compass. Tape a T-pin to the 1" mark on a wooden yardstick…this is the compass point. Tape a sharpened pencil to the 34" mark on the yardstick. With the pin on **A**, draw a curved line between the **AB** and **AC** lines; draw a dotted cutting line ½" beyond this line. Now, cut out the pattern.

4. Placing the "fold" edge of the pattern on the fold of the fabric, cut 6 pieces from assorted colors of fleece, flannel or corduroy. Unfold the pieces, then sew a line ¼" from each edge on the pieces to keep fabric from stretching.

5. Leaving 2 edges un-sewn for an opening, overlap angled edges ¹/₂", pin, then zig-zag pieces together. Make a ¹/₂" hem along outer edge of the skirt.

6. Use 6 strands of embroidery floss to work *Running Stitches*, page 135, around the skirt 3" above the hem. Sew buttons along the stitched line at 5" intervals.

FRINGED WREATH AND TREES
(shown on page 53)
For the wreath, cut an 8"x13" rectangle at the center of a 12"x19" rectangle of 3" thick plastic foam. Use spray adhesive to cover the entire wreath with green felt.

For each tree base, apply glossy wood-tone spray to a wooden round bun leg (like on some sofas) or to 2 wooden discs glued together. Glue a plastic foam cone to the leg.

For the wreath and the tree, cut 2" wide strips from 2 shades of green fleece. Cutting to within ¹/₂" of the opposite long edge and at ¹/₂" intervals, make clips in one long edge for fringe. Alternating shades of green and gluing uncut edge of fringe as you go, wrap fringe through the center and around the wreath until the entire wreath is covered, or beginning at the bottom and working up, wrap fringe around the tree…with each wrap, overlap the uncut edge of the fringe so that the fringe is really dense and the uncut edges do not show. To attach each button, thread one button onto a long straight pin with a head; dip bottom of pin in glue, then stick it into the wreath or tree.

To finish the wreath, make 3 **Heart Felt Ornaments**, page 126, like the instructions indicate. For the large heart, cut the red heart ¹/₂" larger than the heart pattern, then follow the rest of the instructions. Arrange and pin the hearts on the wreath. For the hanger, glue an eye bolt in each top corner on the back of the wreath. Attach craft wire to the eye bolts.

PERSONALIZED FELT BAGS
(shown on page 53)
Refer to Embroidery Stitches, page 135, for sewing how-to's from your Country Friends®. Use 3 strands of floss for all stitching unless otherwise indicated.

For each bag, trace the bag and heart nameplate patterns from page 155 onto tracing paper…or, for a rectangle nameplate, draw a 1¹/₂"x3" pattern on paper. Use the bag pattern to cut a front from felt. Use the heart or rectangle pattern to cut a nameplate from felt; cut a backing for the nameplate ¹/₄" larger all around than the pattern from another color of felt. Lightly pencil the name on the nameplate, then work *Backstitches* over the drawn lines. Place the nameplate on the backing, then work *Running Stitches* along the nameplate edges. Place the nameplate on the front and work *Blanket Stitches* along the edges to attach it.

Pin the front to fur fleece; cut the fleece even with the top of the front piece and ¹/₄" larger on the sides and bottom. Work *Blanket Stitches* along the front edges. Sew a wooden button to each top corner of the bag.

For the handle, thread 20mm red and 11x12mm natural wooden beads onto a 24" piece of 14-gauge green wire…curl the wire around a pen to make loops between some of the beads. Thread each end of the handle through the buttons on the front of the bag and curl wires to secure them in place.

BOX FLOOR CUSHIONS
(shown on page 54)
Whether you use them for extra seating atop the coffee table or for floor seating while unwrapping gifts on Christmas morning, fleece covered pillows will add cozy comfort to all your holiday gatherings.

For each pillow, start with 1¹/₄ yards of polar fleece…cut two 25" squares and two 6"x50" strips from the fleece. For the side gusset, sew the ends of the strips together to form a circle.

Matching right sides and raw edges and placing the seams of the side gusset at opposite corners, pin the side gusset to one of the squares. Using a ¹/₂" seam allowance, sew the pieces together. Leaving one edge open for turning, repeat to attach the remaining square to the pillow cover. Clip the corners and turn the cover right-side out.

To create the "boxed" edges, flatten and pin the side gusset to the square, then sew a ¹/₂" seam around the square…do not sew the seam along the opening edge.

(continued on page 128)

For the cushion, wrap a 22" square of 4" thick foam rubber with several layers of quilt batting. Place the cushion in a plastic bag. Insert the cushion, bag opening end first, into the cover and adjust the cover on the cushion. Carefully slide the bag out of the cover. Pin the opening closed with raw edges folded in ¹/₂". Sew opening closed and hand stitch fleece edges together to finish boxed edge.

Follow manufacturer's instructions to cover four 1¹/₂" diameter buttons with a coordinating fleece. Beginning on the bottom side of pillow, use an upholstery needle and several strands of carpet thread to sew through a plastic 1" diameter button that coordinates with the cover, up through the pillow, through the covered button, then back down through the pillow and the regular button. Pull the threads and tightly knot together to secure.

LIP BALMS
(shown on page 59)
• ¹/₂ oz. refined beeswax
• 4 oz. sweet almond oil
• 1 t. liquid colorant
• 2 t. essential oil
• lip balm tubes and pots
• craft corrugated cardboard
• card stock
• craft glue
• raffia

Combine first 3 ingredients together in a glass bowl and microwave until melted. Stir to blend thoroughly. Add oil to mixture and mix thoroughly; allow to cool slightly, then pour into tubes and pots. Make a corrugated cardboard sleeve for each tube...glue on an oval label cut from card stock. Glue a cardboard circle to the top of each pot...add a square label cut from card stock. Knot raffia around each container. Makes about 8 pots and 8 tubes.

EMBELLISHED TOWEL ENSEMBLE

(shown on page 60)
• matching bath towel, hand towel and washcloth with decorative band on each
• 1¹/₂" wide embossed ribbon
• ¹/₂" wide crocheted trim same color as towels
• clear nylon thread
• ³/₄" wide ribbon
• assorted shank buttons

Use machine washable ribbons, trims and buttons.

1. For each towel, overlapping ribbon ends to back of towel, pin a length of embossed ribbon across towel over one decorative band of the towel. Pin lengths of trim along and just below edges of embossed ribbon; use clear thread to sew ribbon and trim in place.

2. Wrapping ends to back of towel and centering ribbon along embossed ribbon, gather or twist ³/₄" wide ribbon every 1¹/₂" along embossed ribbon. Sew a button through each gather or twist...be sure to stitch through ribbon and towel. Sew ribbon ends to towel.

3. For the washcloth, wrapping ends to back of cloth and centering ribbon along decorative band on cloth, gather or twist ³/₄" wide ribbon every 1¹/₂" along the band. Sew a button through each ribbon twist or gather, being sure to stitch through the ribbon and washcloth. Sew ribbon ends to secure.

WARMING NECK COZY
(shown on page 60)
• muslin
• hand towel with decorative band
• 4 lbs. uncooked rice
• 1¹/₂" wide embossed ribbon
• ³/₄" wide ribbon
• assorted shank buttons
• clear nylon thread
• hoop and loop fastener dots

Use a ¹/₂" seam allowance for all sewing unless otherwise indicated.

1. For the rice bag, cut a piece of muslin the same size as the towel. Sew long edges together, then one end. Turn bag right-side out. Matching ends, fold bag in half; lightly mark along fold. Open bag and fold one end to drawn line and mark along that fold. Repeat for other end...this divides the bag into 4 sections and allows the rice to stay evenly distributed. Pour one pound of rice in bag; sew along drawn line. Repeat to fill and sew each section.

2. Omitting the trim, follow Steps 1 and 2 of the **Embellished Towel Ensemble** to attach ribbons and buttons over both decorative bands on the towel.

3. For the bag cover, matching right sides and long edges, fold towel in half; leaving a 12" opening at center, sew long edges together. With the seam at center back, sew across each end. Clip corners and turn right-side out.

4. Sew one edge ¹/₂" to the wrong side. Sew fasteners along opening. Insert rice bag into cover and close fasteners.

LOVELY TRIMMED ROBE
(shown on page 64)

- woman's long-sleeve robe with a shawl collar
- 6" wide toile ribbon (we used wire-edged ribbon and removed the wires)
- coordinating crocheted trim with a flange
- coordinating handkerchief
- shank button

1. Turn the robe wrong-side out. For each decorative cuff, measure around the cuff and add 1"; cut a length of ribbon this length. Press one end of the ribbon ½" to the wrong side. With unpressed end of ribbon along seamline on cuff, wrap and pin the ribbon around cuff. Topstitch ribbon to cuff along edges and down pressed end over seam. Turn robe right-side out.

2. To make the pocket, cut a 6½" length of ribbon; press one end (bottom) ½" to wrong side. For flap, refer to Fig. 1 to place pocket on wrong side of handkerchief. Cut corner from handkerchief ½" above top of pocket; trim side points of flap ½" from edges of pocket.

Fig. 1

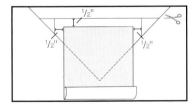

3. Sew trim along point of flap. Matching wrong sides and overlapping edges of flap and pocket ½", sew across top of pocket (Fig. 2). Press flap to right side, then press

edges of flap to wrong side of pocket. Pin pocket to robe and top stitch along side and bottom edges. Sew a button on the point of the flap.

Fig. 2

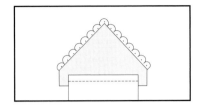

4. Press cut edge of ribbon ¼" to the wrong side. Matching center back of collar with center of ribbon length and inserting flange of trim between ribbon and collar so ribbon extends past edge of collar, pin pressed edge of ribbon and trim along outer edges of collar.

5. Easing ribbon to fit, pin finished edge of ribbon along inner edges of collar.

6. Trim bottom edges of ribbon ½" past bottom edge of collar; fold edges under and pin in place. Topstitch along each end to secure in place.

VINTAGE HANDBAG
(shown on page 65)

- 4"x7" piece of handkerchief with finished edge
- 7"x15" piece of corduroy for purse
- 3½" length of 2" wide ribbon
- 7"x15" piece of cotton fabric for lining
- vintage beads
- 12" of 24-gauge wire
- wire cutters
- medium-duty snap
- shank button

1. Matching raw edges, pin handkerchief piece, right-side up, to right side of one end of corduroy piece; baste in place.

2. Press one end of ribbon ½" to the wrong side twice; tack in place. Pinch ribbon above hem; wrap thread around gathers to hold them in place. Matching right sides, center and pin the un-hemmed end of the ribbon to the end of the corduroy opposite the handkerchief.

3. Matching right sides and ends and leaving top open, sew sides of corduroy piece together; press, then turn right-side out. Repeat with lining fabric piece; do not turn right-side out.

4. Matching raw edges, place corduroy in lining. Leaving an opening for turning, sew top edges together. Turn bag right-side out, tucking lining into bag; sew opening closed.

5. For handle, sew two beads to each corner of bag. Wrap one end of the wire length around one bead on bag and twist end around itself to secure. Thread beads onto wire length to about 1" from end. Repeat previous to secure wire to bead on opposite corner of bag; trim excess wire.

6. Sew one side of snap to ribbon and remaining side to purse. Sew button over gathered part of ribbon.

HOME RUN CLOCK
(shown on page 66)
Hit a home run with this gift for Dad! And, the clock keeps time until the next game!

- 8"x10" frame with backing (without glass)
- 8"x10" piece of corrugated kraft paper
- red and blue card stock
- craft glue
- three 2"x3" photos of child playing baseball
- 3"x3½" photo of dad and child
- three 2⅜"x4¾" cargo tags
- black permanent marker
- 3 star-shaped eyelets
- drill and bits
- battery-operated clock kit
- 4 baseball stickers
- easel

1. Remove backing from frame; place corrugated paper in frame, then replace backing.

2. Cut three 2¼"x3¼" "mats" from red card stock for the small photos. Cut one 3¼"x3¾" red and one 3½"x4" blue mat from card stock for the larger photo.

3. Stack and glue the small photos on the mats, then the mats on the tags; glue the large photo on the red mat, then the red mat on the blue mat. Use the marker to write "D-a-a-d!", "Hit it!" and "Run!" on the tags below the photos, then glue eyelets over the holes in the tags. Arrange and glue mats and tags on the cardboard in the frame.

4. Follow manufacturer's instructions to mount the clock in the frame. Place baseball stickers at the 12, 3, 6, and 9 o'clock positions. Place the clock on the easel.

DAD'S TRAVEL MUG
(shown on page 67)
A handpainted magnet makes the perfect adornment on a new steel mug for dad! (Just remove the magnet before washing the mug.)

Cut a circle from a self-adhesive magnetic sheet to fit on the mug. Swirl together blue and white paint on the circle for the ocean; when dry, draw shapes for the continents and the outer edges of the banner across the circle. Mix green and white paints to fill in the continent shapes and paint the banner red. Paint white grid lines to resemble a globe. Use a black marker to write "WORLD'S BEST DAD" across the banner and to outline the banner and continents.

CROCHET SLIPPERS
(continued from page 68)
SLIPPER SOLE
With Red, ch 26.

Rnd 1 (Right side): 2 Sc in second ch from hook, sc in next 10 chs, hdc in next 3 chs, dc in next 8 chs, 2 dc in next ch, hdc in next ch, 5 sc in last ch (toe); working in free loops of beginning ch **(Fig. 1, page 134)**, hdc in next ch, 2 dc in next ch, dc in next 8 chs, hdc in next 3 chs, sc in next 10 chs, 2 sc in same ch as first sc; do **not** join; place marker **(see Markers, page 134)**: 57 sts.

Note: Loop a short piece of yarn around any stitch to mark Rnd 1 as **right** side.

Rnd 2: 2 Sc in each of next 2 sc, sc in next 24 sts, 2 sc in next sc, (sc in next sc, 2 sc in next sc) twice, sc in next 24 sts, 2 sc in each of next 2 sc: 64 sc.

Rnd 3: Sc in next sc, 2 sc in next sc, sc in next 25 sc, 2 sc in next sc, (sc in next 2 sc, 2 sc in next sc) 3 times, sc in next 25 sc, 2 sc in next sc, sc in next sc: 70 sc.

Rnd 4: Sc in next sc, 2 sc in next sc, sc in next 28 sc, 2 sc in next sc, (sc in next 2 sc, 2 sc in next sc) 3 times, sc in next 28 sc, 2 sc in next sc, sc in next sc: 76 sc.

Rnd 5: Sc in next 36 sc, 2 sc in next sc, sc in next 4 sc, 2 sc in next sc, sc in each sc around; do **not** finish off: 78 sc.

SIDES
Rnds 1-5: Sc in each sc around.

Rnd 6: Sc in next 36 sc, place marker around last sc made for Instep placement, sc in each sc around; slip st in next sc, finish off.

INSTEP
Row 1: With **right** side facing, join Red with slip st in marked sc on Rnd 6 of Sides; work beginning dc decrease, dc in next 6 sc, work dc decrease, sc in next sc, leave remaining sc unworked: 9 sts.

Row 2: Ch 1, turn; skip first sc, sc in next 8 dc, work sc decrease: 9 sc.

Row 3: Ch 1, turn; skip first sc, sc in next 8 sc on Instep, work sc decrease.

Rows 4 and 5: Ch 1, turn; skip first sc, sc in next 8 sc on Instep, sc in next sc on Sides.

Rows 6 and 7: Ch 1, turn; skip first sc, sc in next 8 sc on Instep, work sc decrease.

Rows 8 and 9: Ch 1, turn; skip first sc, sc in next 8 sc on Instep, sc in next sc on Sides.

Rows 10 and 11: Ch 1, turn; skip first sc, sc in next 8 sc on Instep, work sc decrease.

Row 12: Ch 1, turn; skip first sc, sc in next 8 sc on Instep, sc in next sc on Sides; finish off.

CUFF
Rnd 1: With wrong side facing, join White with sc in same st as joining slip st on Rnd 6 of Sides (see **Joining With Sc, page 134**); sc in each sc across Sides to Instep, sc in first 8 sc on Row 12 of Instep, skip last sc, sc in each sc across Sides; join with slip st to first sc: 56 sc.

Rnd 2: Do **not** turn; work Loop Stitch in each sc around (**Figs. 2a-2c, page 134**): 56 Loop Sts.

Rnds 3-14: Work Loop Stitch in each Loop Stitch around.

Rnd 15: Slip st tightly in each Loop Stitch around, finish off leaving a long end for sewing.

Cut all loops and brush to resemble fur. Fold Cuff to wrong side and sew to Rnd 1 of Cuff.

KNIT SOCKS
(shown on page 69)
Size Note: Instructions are written for size Small with sizes Medium and Large in braces { }. Instructions will be easier to read if you circle all the numbers pertaining to your size. If only one number is given, it applies to all sizes.

FINISHED FOOT CIRCUMFERENCE
SMALL	MEDIUM	LARGE
7½"	8"	8½"

MATERIALS
Fingering Weight Yarn:
      400 yards
      (366 meters)
Double pointed knitting needles, sizes 1 (2.25 mm) and 2 (2.75 mm) (sets of 5) or sizes needed for gauge
Markers
Stitch holder
Tapesty needle

GAUGE: With smaller size needles, in **Stockinette**, Stitch 28 sts and 36 rows = 4" (10 cm)

CUFF
With larger size needles cast on 52{56-60} sts. Divide sts evenly onto 4 double pointed needles (see **Double Pointed Needles, page 136**), place marker at beginning of round (see **Markers, page 136**), join.

Work in K2, P2 ribbing for 2" (5 cm).

Knit each round until Cuff measures approximately 3¼{3½-3¾}"/8.5{9-9.5} cm, from cast on edge.

Changing to smaller size needles, knit each round until Cuff measures approximately 6½{7-7½}"/16.5{18-19} cm, from cast on edge.

Slip last 26{28-30} sts worked on stitch holder to work Instep later: 26{28-30} sts.

HEEL FLAP
Row 1: (Slip 1 as if to purl wyb, K1) across working sts onto one needle.

Row 2: (Slip 1 as if to purl wyf, P1) across.

Repeat Rows 1 and 2 until Heel Flap measures approximately 2¾{3-3¼}"/7{7.5-8.5} cm, ending by working Row 2.

TURN HEEL
Begin working in short rows as follows:

Row 1: Knit across to last 11 sts, SSK, K1, turn, leave last 8 sts unworked: 17{19-21} sts.

Row 2 (Right side): Slip 1, P6{8-10}, P2 tog, P1, turn: 8{10-12} sts.

Row 3: Slip 1, K7{9-11}, SSK, K1, turn: 9{11-13} sts.

Row 4: Slip 1, P8{10-12}, P2 tog, P1, turn: 10{12-14} sts.

Repeat Rows 3 and 4 adding one st before decrease until all Heel sts have been worked, ending by working right side row: 16{18-20} sts.

GUSSET
Knit 9{10-11} sts; place marker (this is now the end of rnd marker); with another needle, knit 9{10-11} sts, pick up 19{21-23} sts along edge of Heel Flap, place marker, (with another needle, knit 14{16-18} sts of instep) twice; place marker, with another needle, pick up 19{21-23} sts along edge of Heel Flap, knit 9{10-11} sts: 79{88-97}.

Rnd 1: Knit around.

Rnd 2: Knit around to within 3 sts of first marker, K2 tog, K1, slip marker, knit to second marker, slip marker, K1, SSK, knit around.

(continued on page 132)

Repeat Rnds 1 and 2 until 52{56-60} sts remain.

Note: Keep markers in place for Toe shaping.

FOOT
Work even knitting each round until Foot measures approximately 6$\frac{1}{2}${7$\frac{1}{2}$-8}"/16.5{19-20.5} cm from back of heel or 1$\frac{3}{4}${2-2}"/4.5{5-5} cm less than total desired Foot length from back of Heel.

TOE
Rnd 1: Knit around to within 3 sts of first marker, K2 tog, K1, slip marker, K1, SSK, knit around to within 3 sts of second marker, K2 tog, K1, slip marker, K1, SSK, knit around.

Rnd 2: Knit around.

Repeat Rnds 1 and 2 until 20 sts remain.

FINISHING
Knit across first 5 sts of rnd. 10 sts will be for the top of foot and 10 sts will be for the bottom of the foot. Graft remaining stitches together (Fig. 1a and 1b).

GRAFTING
Stitches to be woven are held on two knitting needles, with one behind the other and wrong sides together. Threaded yarn needle should be on right side of work. Work in the following sequence, pulling yarn through as if to knit or as if to purl with even tension and keeping yarn under points of needles to avoid tangling and extra loops.

Step 1: Purl first stitch on front needle, leave on (Fig. 1a).
Step 2: Knit first stitch on back needle, leave on (Fig. 1b).
Step 3: Knit first stitch on front needle, slip off.
Step 4: Purl next stitch on front needle, leave on.
Step 5: Purl first stitch on back needle, slip off.
Step 6: Knit next stitch on back needle, leave on.
Repeat Steps 3-6 across until all stitches are worked off the needles.

Fig. 1a	Fig. 1b

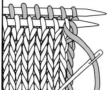 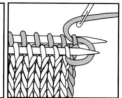

DOGGIE SWEATER
(shown on page 70)
Using the sweater pattern on page 157, refer to *Making Patterns*, page 133, to make an entire pattern…be sure to cut off the neck piece from **one side** of the pattern as indicated on the pattern. You can reduce or enlarge the pattern on a photocopier, then size the pattern to you dog to make sure it fits. Use the pattern to cut a sweater from fleece.

Drape the sweater over your dog and measure across his belly from one bottom edge of the sweater to the other; add 5" to the measurement, then cut a 5$\frac{1}{2}$" wide strap from fleece the determined measurement. Matching ends, fold the strap in half, then cut it along the fold…this will give you 2 short straps! To finish each strap, fold the strap in half

lengthwise; stitch along the long edge and across one end. Turn the strap right-side out and topstitch along the edges.

Pin the edges of the sweater $\frac{1}{2}$" to the wrong side, then zig-zag in place. Sew the open end of each strap to the wrong side of the jacket as indicated on the pattern.

Sew hook and loop fasteners to the straps and the front closure.

BEADED AND WIRED BASKET
(shown on page 74)
Spray paint an oval-shaped basket a bright Christmasy red.

For the tag, use red alphabet stickers to spell out a message on a rectangle of cream card stock. Glue the rectangle to green card stock and cut $\frac{1}{4}$" larger than the rectangle. Attach star-shaped red eyelets to top corners of the tag.

Randomly thread green plastic pony and berry beads and red plastic starburst beads onto a really long length of red plastic-coated 22-gauge craft wire. Leaving long tales at the beginning and end, randomly releasing a bead at a time and twisting and curling the wire before and after to hold each bead in place, and beginning at front of basket, weave wire in and out of openings in the basket under the rim.

Thread tag onto wire ends; curl wires, add a bead and curl end of wires to secure tag to basket.

Line the basket with cream-colored shredded paper. Nestle cellophane bags of cookies tied with lengths of red curled wire and beads in the basket.

APRON
(shown on page 80)
- 17"x20" piece of fabric for apron
- 6½" square of fabric for pocket
- 60" of 2"w bias binding strip for apron and pocket trim (pieced as necessary)
- 80" of 6"w bias binding strip for apron ties trim (pieced as necessary)
- 7" of jumbo rick-rack

1. Matching short edges, fold the apron fabric in half. Using a plate as a guide, mark and cut rounded bottom corners. Repeat to round the bottom corners of the pocket.

2. For narrow and wide binding, match wrong sides and press bias strips in half. Unfold and press long edges to center fold. For wide binding only, press ends of strip ¼" to wrong side. Refold strips.

3. Cut a 7" piece of narrow binding. Pin top edge of pocket in fold of binding piece. Catching front and back edges of binding in stitching, top stitch in place. Sew rick-rack over edge of binding. Press raw edges of pocket ¼" to wrong side. Sew pocket to apron.

4. Pin bottom edge of apron in fold of narrow binding. Catching front and back edges of binding in stitching, top stitch in place…trim binding even with top edge of apron.

5. Matching center of apron to center of wide binding, pin top edge of apron in fold of binding. Catching front and back edges of binding in stitching, top stitch along ends and across bottom edge.

JOY BOX
(shown on page 84)
Paint an oval-shaped paper-maché box and a puffy wooden star with white primer. When they're dry, use a diamond-shaped sponge to stamp a beige-color argyle pattern across the lid. Paint the edges of the lid and star with the beige paint. Use a piece of natural sponge to stamp peach-color paint over the box, lid and star. Use a black paint pen to write "Joy!" on the star, then glue the star to the center of the lid. Lightly brush the star and area around the star with glitter paint. Use an ultra-fine black permanent marker to write a wavy string of your favorite Christmas carol titles along the top edge of the lid and around the sides of the box.

GENERAL INSTRUCTIONS

MAKING PATTERNS

When the entire pattern is shown, place tracing paper over the pattern and draw over lines. For a more durable pattern, use a permanent marker to draw over pattern on stencil plastic.

When patterns are stacked or over-lapped, place tracing paper over the pattern and follow a single colored line to trace the pattern. Repeat to trace each pattern separately onto tracing paper.

When tracing a two-part pattern, draw over the first part of the pattern onto tracing paper, then match the dashed lines and arrows and draw over the second part of the pattern onto the tracing paper.

When only half of the pattern is shown (indicated by a solid blue line on pattern), fold the tracing paper in half. Place the fold along the solid blue line and trace pattern half; turn folded paper over and draw over the traced lines on the remaining side. Unfold the pattern; cut out.

MAKING A TAG OR LABEL

For a quick & easy tag or label, photocopy or trace (use transfer paper to transfer design) a copyright-free design onto card stock…or just cut a shape from card stock. Color tag with colored pencils, crayons or thinned acrylic paint; draw over transferred lines using permanent markers or paint pens. Use straight-edge or decorative-edge craft scissors to cut out tag; glue to colored or decorative paper or card stock, then cut tag out, leaving a border around it. Use a pen or marker to write a message on the tag. You can also choose items from a wide variety of self-adhesive stickers, borders or frames; rubber stamps and inkpads; or gel pens in an assortment of colors, densities and point-widths to further embellish your tags or labels.

CROCHET
ABBREVIATIONS

ch(s)	chain(s)
cm	centimeters
dc	double crochet(s)
hdc	half double crochet(s)
mm	millimeters
Rnd(s)	Round(s)
sc	single crochet(s)
sp(s)	space(s)
st(s)	stitch(es)
YO	yarn over

— work instructions following as many more times as indicated in addition to the first time.

( )— work enclosed instructions as many times as specified by the number immediately following or work all enclosed instructions in the stitch or space indicated or contains explanatory remarks.

colon (:) — the number(s) given after a colon at the end of a row or round denote(s) the number of stitches or spaces you should have on that row or round.

GAUGE

Exact gauge is essential for proper fit. Before beginning your project, make the sample swatch given in the individual instructions in the yarn and hook specified.

After completing the swatch, measure it, counting your stitches and rows or rounds carefully. If your swatch is larger or smaller than specified, make another, changing hook size to get the correct gauge. Keep trying until you find the size hook that will give you the specified gauge.

MARKERS

Markers are used to help distinguish the beginning of each round being worked. Place a 2" (5 cm) scrap piece of yarn before the first stitch of each round, moving marker after each round is complete.

JOINING WITH SC

When instructed to join with sc, begin with a slip knot on hook. Insert hook in stitch or space indicated, YO and pull up a loop, YO and draw through both loops on hook.

FREE LOOPS OF A CHAIN

When instructed to work in free loops of a chain, work in loop indicated by arrow (Fig. 1).

Fig. 1

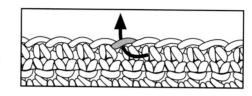

LOOP STITCH

Insert hook in next stitch, wrap yarn around index finger of left hand once, insert hook through all loops on finger following direction indicated by arrow (Fig. 2a), being careful to hook all loops (Fig. 2b), draw through st, remove finger from loops, YO and draw through all 3 loops on hook pulling each loop to measure approximately 1½" (Loop St made, Fig. 2c).

Fig. 2a   **Fig. 2b**

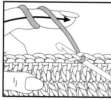   

Fig. 2c

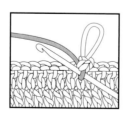

NO SLIP FINISHING

To provide traction on bottom Sole of each Slipper, use fabric paint to add rows of wavy lines or dots as desired to heel and toe; let paint dry completely.

MAKING A BOW

1. For first streamer, measure desired length of streamer from one end of ribbon; twist ribbon between fingers as shown in Fig. 1.

2. Keeping right side of ribbon facing out, fold ribbon to front to form desired-size loop; gather ribbon between fingers (Fig. 2). Fold ribbon to bak to form another loop; gather ribbon between fingers (Fig. 3).

3. If center loop is desired, form half the desired number of loops, then loosely wrap ribbon around thumb and gather ribbon between fingers as shown in Fig. 4; form remaining loops. Continue to form loops; varying size of loops as desired, until bow is desired size.

Fig. 1   **Fig. 2**

Fig. 3   **Fig. 4**

   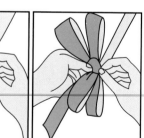

4. For remaining streamer, trim ribbon to desired length.

5. To secure bow, hold gathered loops tightly. Fold a length of floral wire around gathers of loops. Hold wire ends behind bow, gathering all loops forward; twist bow to tighten wire. Arrange loops and trim ribbon ends as desired.

LETTERING

For unique and personal labels or lettering on your crafts, use one of your favorite fonts from your computer...try the "bold" and "italic" buttons for different variations of the font. Size your words to fit your project, then print them out. Using your printout as the pattern, use transfer paper to transfer the words to your project. If you're making appliqué letters, you'll need to trace the letters in reverse, onto the paper side of fusible web. Don't forget about the old-reliable lettering stencils...they're easy to use and come in a wide variety of styles and sizes. And, if you're already into memory page making, you probably have an alphabet set or 2 of rubber letter stamps...just select an inkpad type suitable for your project. Then, there are 100's of sizes, colors and shapes of sticker and rub-on letters...small, fat, shiny, flat, puffy, velvety, slick, smooth, rough...you get the idea! Only your imagination limits you.

EMBROIDERY STITCHES

Preparing floss: If your project will be laundered, soak floss in a mixture of one cup water and one tablespoon vinegar for a few minutes and allow to dry before using to prevent colors from bleeding or fading.

Backstitch: Referring to Fig. 1, bring needle up at 1; go down at 2; bring up at 3 and pull through. For next stitch, insert needle at 1; bring up at 4 and pull through.

Fig. 1

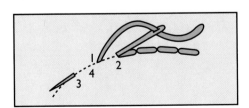

Blanket Stitch: Referring to Fig. 2a, bring needle up at 1. Keeping thread below point of needle, go down at 2 and come up at 3. Continue working as shown in Fig. 2b.

Fig. 2a   **Fig. 2b**

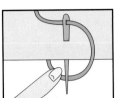 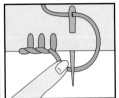

French Knot: Referring to Fig. 3, bring needle up at 1. Wrap floss once around needle and insert needle at 2, holding end of floss with non-stitching fingers.

Fig. 3

Running Stitch: Referring to Fig. 4, make a series of straight stitches with stitch length equal to the space between stitches.

Fig. 4

Satin Stitch: Referring to Fig. 5, come up at odd numbers and go down at even numbers with the stitches touching but not overlapping.

Fig. 5

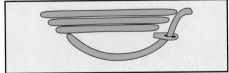

Straight Stitch: Referring to Fig. 6, come up at 1 and go down at 2.

Fig. 6

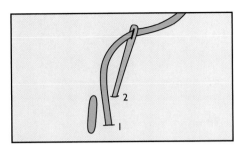

KNIT

ABBREVIATIONS

cm	centimeters
K	knit
mm	millimeters
P	purl
Rnd(s)	Round(s)
SSK	slip, slip, knit
st(s)	stitch(es)
wyb	with yarn in back
wyf	with yarn in front

( ) — work enclosed instructions as many times as specified by the number immediately following or contains explanatory remarks.

colon (:) — the number(s) given after a colon at the end of a row or round denote(s) the number of stitches or spaces you should have on that row or round.

work even — work without increasing or decreasing in the established pattern.

GAUGE

Exact gauge is essential for proper fit. Before beginning your sock, make swatch in the yarn and needle specified. After completing the swatch, measure it, counting your stitches and rows carefully. If your swatch is larger or smaller than specified, make another, changing needle size to get the correct gauge. Keep trying until you find the size needles that will give you the specified gauge.

(continued on page 136)

MARKERS

As a convenience to you, we have used markers to help distinguish the beginning of a round. Place markers as instructed. You may use purchased markers or tie a length of contrasting color yarn around the needle. When you reach a marker on each row, slip it from the left needle to the right needle; remove it when no longer needed.

DOUBLE POINTED NEEDLES

Using one double pointed needle, cast on all stitches as instructed. Place a marker to mark beginning of rounds. Divide the number of stitches evenly onto four needles (Fig. 1a) and begin to work with the fifth needle (Fig. 1b). Work the first stitch on each needle firmly to prevent gaps. Work across the first needle as instructed. With an empty needle, work across second, third and fourth needle in same manner. Make sure stitches are not twisted.

Fig. 1a

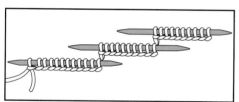

Fig. 1b

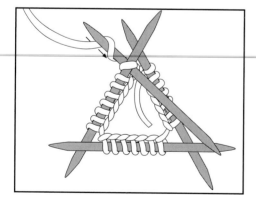

STOCKINETTE STITCH

Knit one row or number of stitches indicated (right side), purl one row or number of stitches indicated. The knit side is smooth and flat (Fig. 2a), and the purl side is bumpy (Fig. 2b).

Fig. 2a   **Fig. 2b**

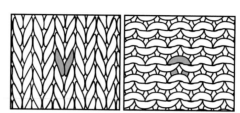

KNIT 2 TOGETHER

(abbreviated K2 tog)

Insert the right needle into the front of the first two stitches on the left needle as if to knit (Fig. 3), then knit them together as if they were one stitch.

Fig. 3

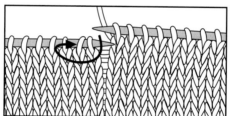

SLIP, SLIP, KNIT

(abbreviated SSK)

With yarn in back of work, separately slip two stitches as if to knit (Fig. 4a). Insert the left needle into the front of both slipped stitches (Fig. 4b) and knit them together (Fig. 4c).

Fig. 4a   **Fig. 4b**

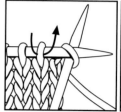

Fig. 4c

PURL 2 TOGETHER

(abbreviated P2 tog)

Insert the right needle into the front of the first two stitches on the left needle as if to purl (Fig. 5), then purl them together as if they were one stitch.

Fig. 5

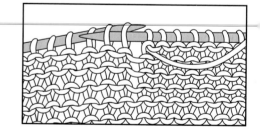

FAMILY MEMORY WREATH
(pages 8 and 9)

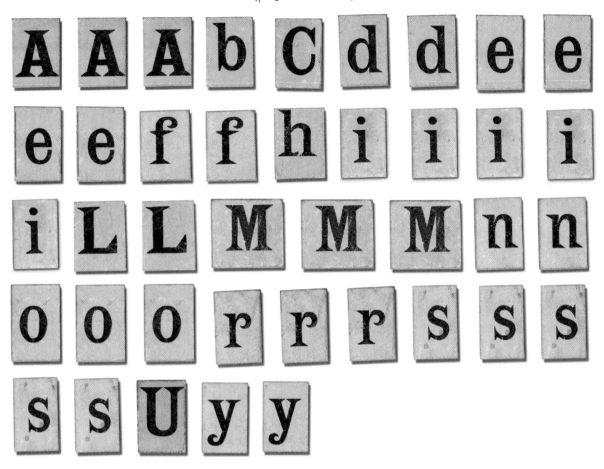

CARD-MAKING PARTY INVITATIONS
(page 22)

Family Christmas Memories

WISHES JOURNAL
(page 13)

BABY'S FIRST STOCKING
(page 18)

ADVENT COUNTDOWN
(page 19)

139

STORY-TIME SANTA BLANKET

(page 14)

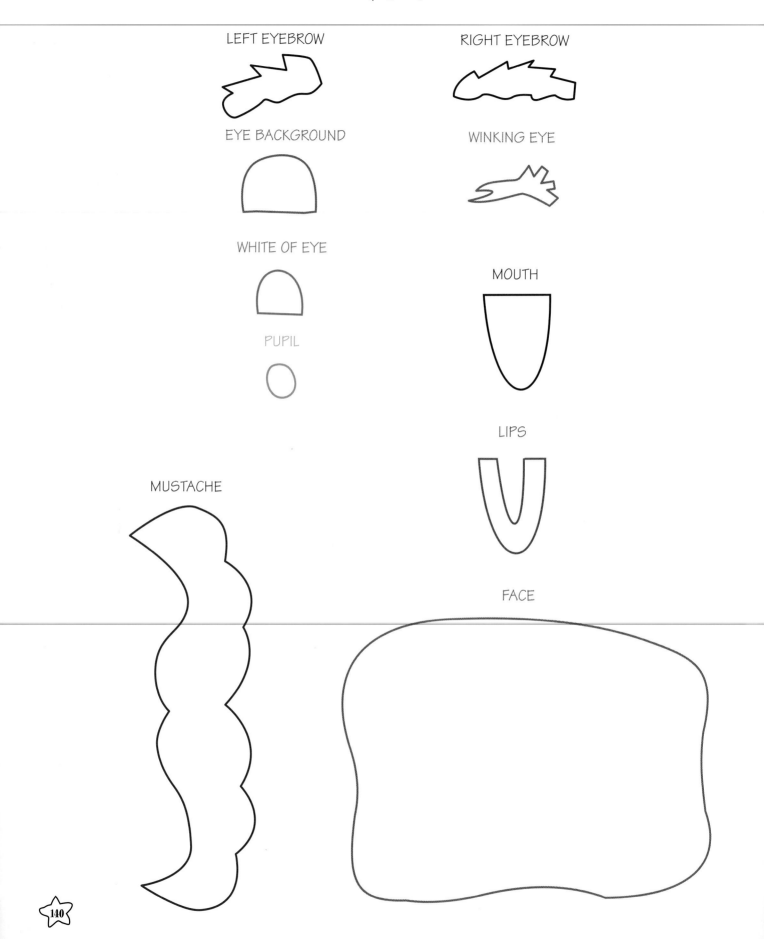

LEFT EYEBROW

RIGHT EYEBROW

EYE BACKGROUND

WINKING EYE

WHITE OF EYE

MOUTH

PUPIL

LIPS

MUSTACHE

FACE

STORY-TIME SANTA BLANKET
(page 14)

POM-POM

HAT

HATBAND

ARGYLE AND HEART FELT ORNAMENTS
(page 52)

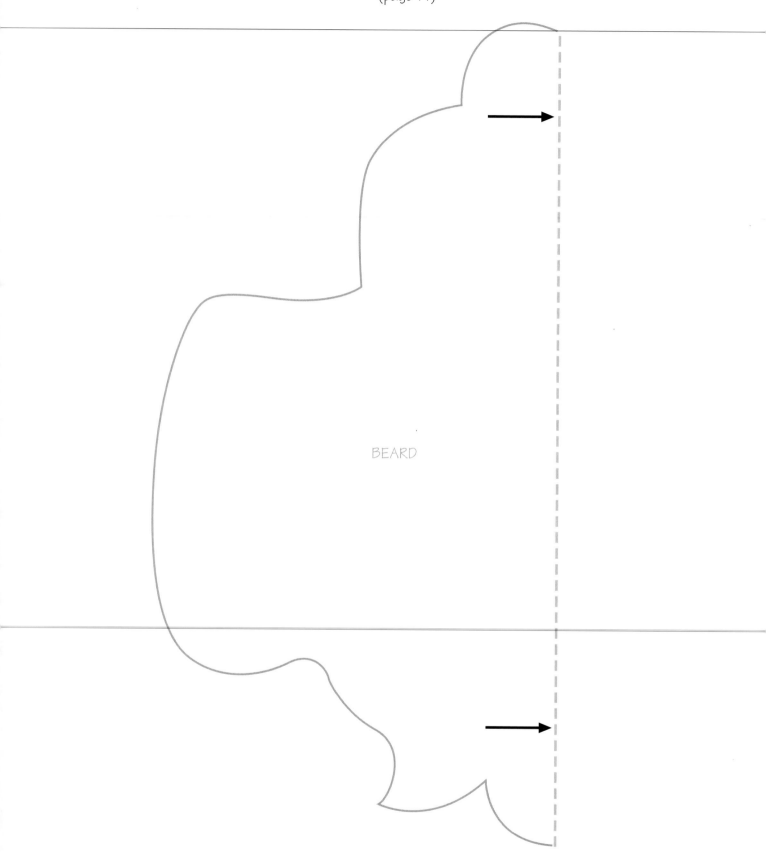

BEARD

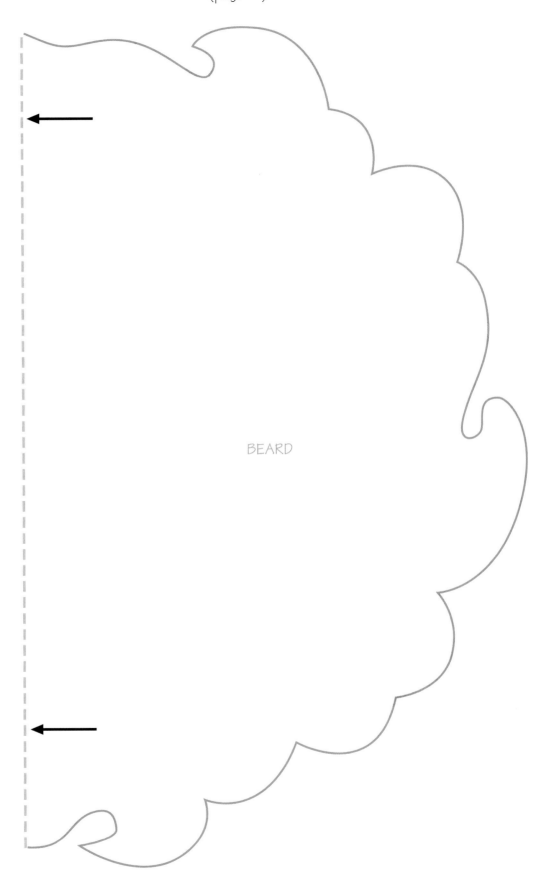

BEARD

GINGERBREAD PANCAKES
(page 80)

How To make

gingerbread pancakes

Place 2 teaspoons instant coffee granules in ¼ cup boiling water; stir 'til dissolved and cool completely. Blend in ⅔ cup milk, one egg and one tablespoon oil; set aside. Add pancake mix to large mixing bowl. Make a well in the center. Pour liquid mixture into the well; stir until just moistened. Heat ¼ cup of batter on a greased griddle until bubbles form along the edge. Flip and heat 'til golden. Makes eight 4-inch pancakes.

CARD-MAKING PARTY INVITATIONS
(page 22)

A Merry Christmas

PEPPERMINTY COCOA MIX
(page 81)

Pepperminty Cocoa Mix

from ....

To make one serving, add 5 to 6 tablespoons of mix to your mug. Add one cup boiling water. Stir.

BATHROOM DÉCOR
(pages 30 and 31)

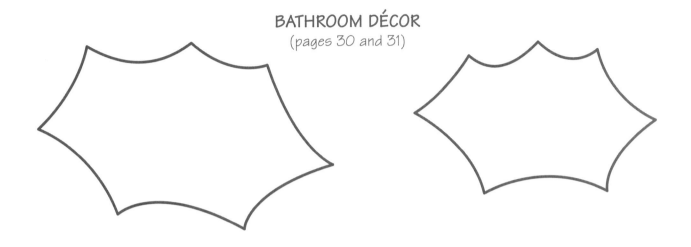

OVERSIZED STOCKING
(page 26)
(enlarge 167%)

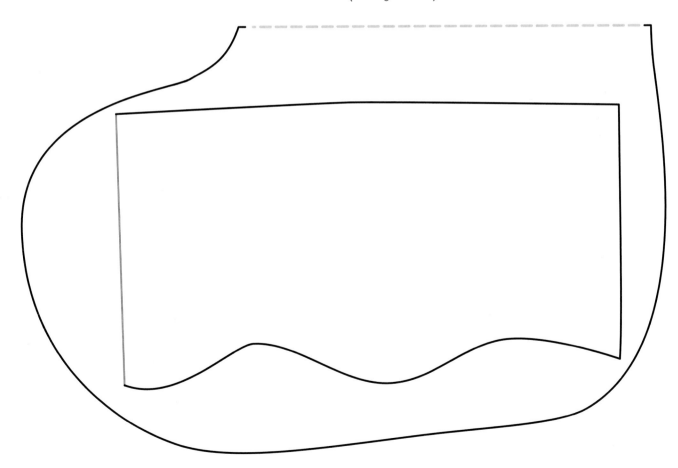

Mrs. Santa

CASSEROLE COZY
(page 35)
(enlarge 167%)

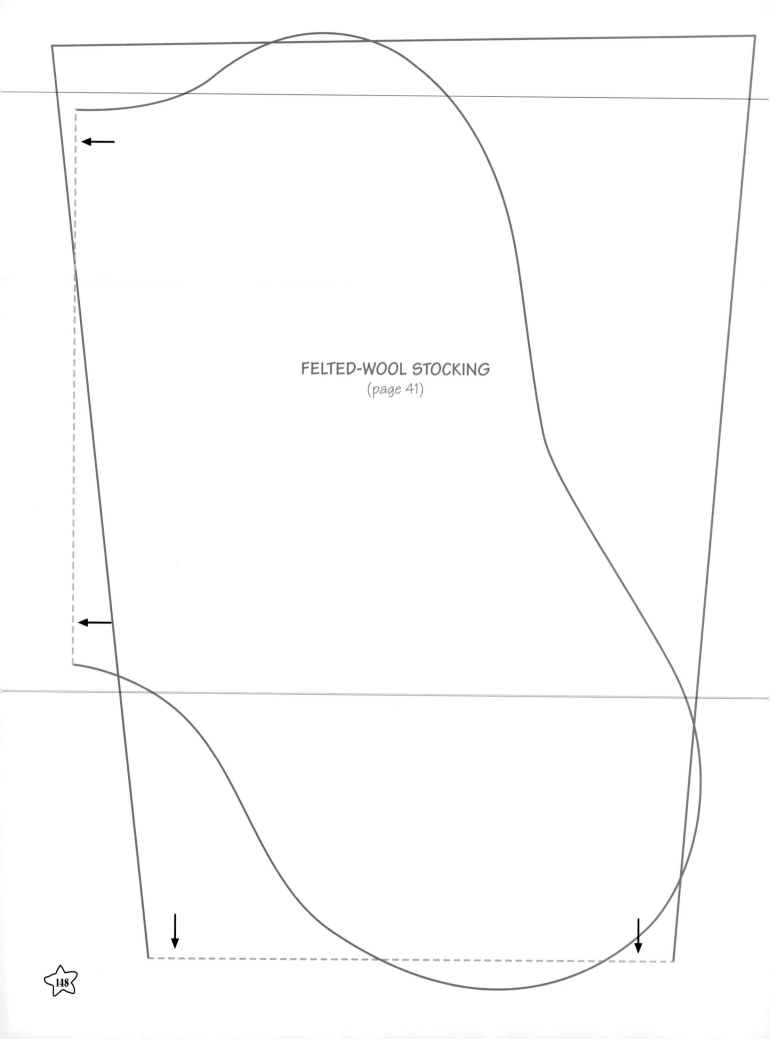

FELTED-WOOL STOCKING
(page 41)

STUFFED TEDDY BEAR
(page 42)

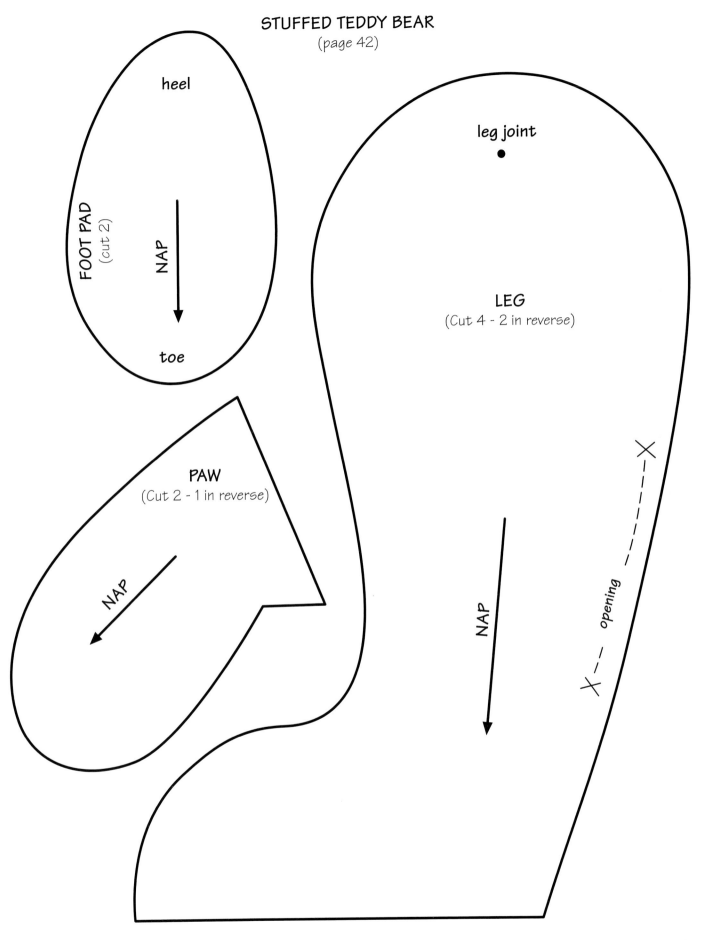

heel

FOOT PAD
(cut 2)

NAP

toe

leg joint

LEG
(Cut 4 - 2 in reverse)

NAP

PAW
(Cut 2 - 1 in reverse)

NAP

opening

STUFFED TEDDY BEAR
(page 43)

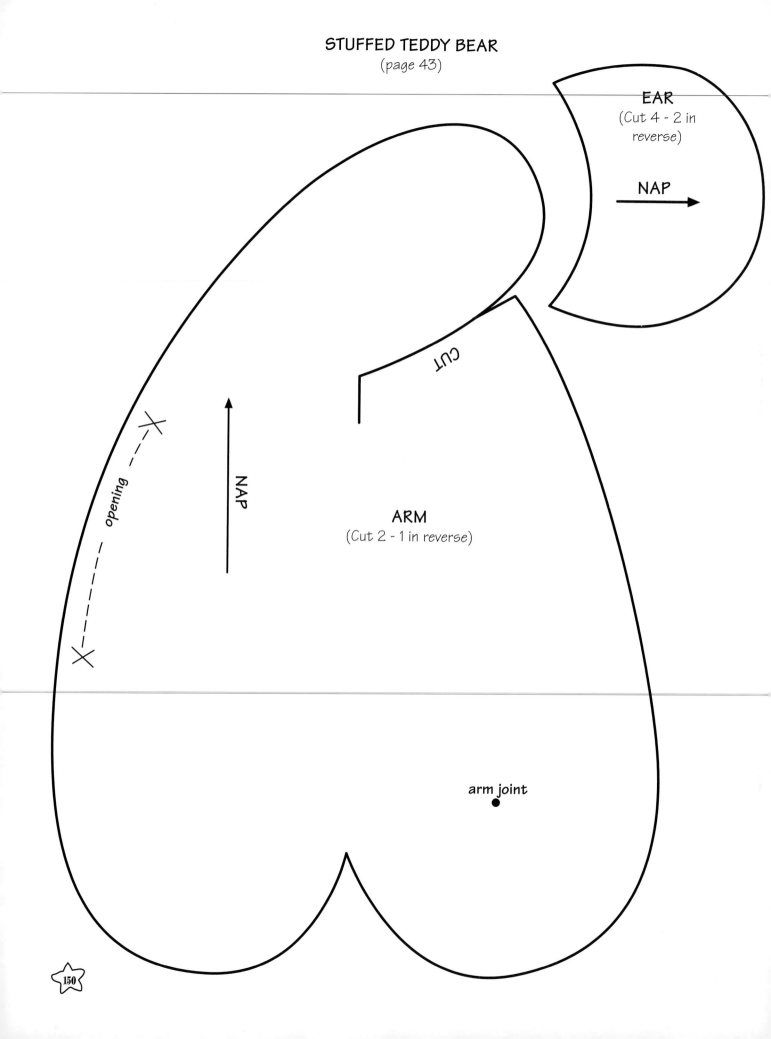

EAR
(Cut 4 - 2 in
reverse)

NAP

CUT

NAP

opening

ARM
(Cut 2 - 1 in reverse)

arm joint

STUFFED TEDDY BEAR
(page 43)

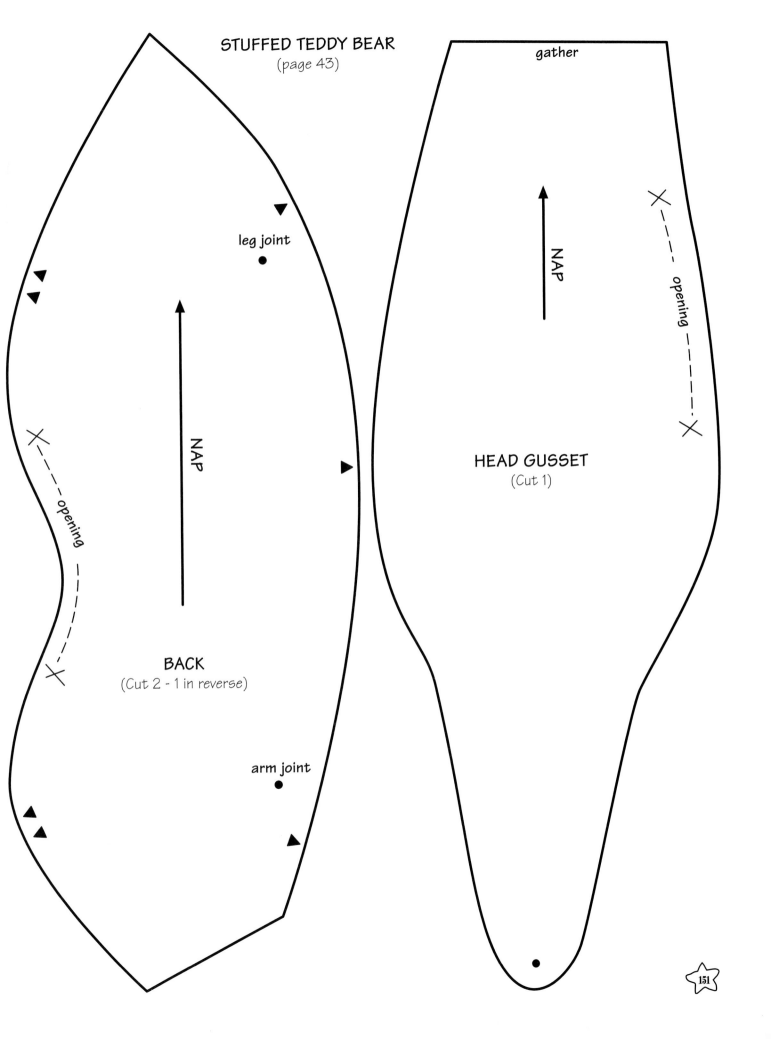

leg joint

NAP

opening

BACK
(Cut 2 - 1 in reverse)

arm joint

gather

NAP

opening

HEAD GUSSET
(Cut 1)

gather

STUFFED TEDDY BEAR
(page 43)

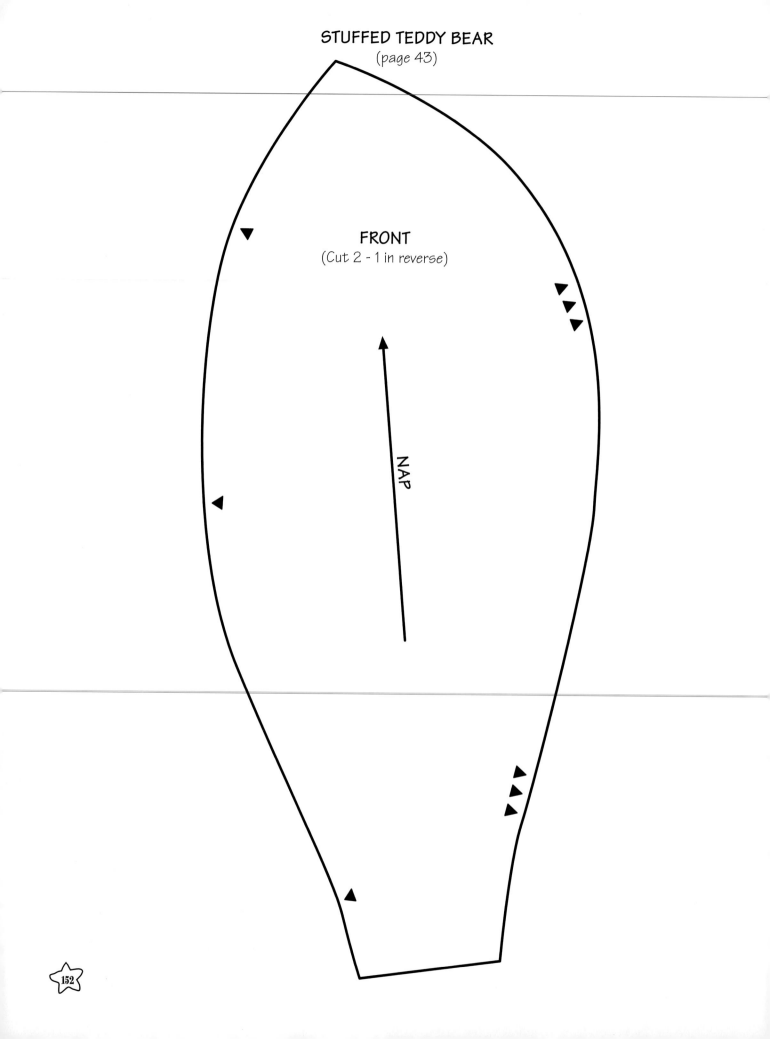

FRONT
(Cut 2 - 1 in reverse)

NAP

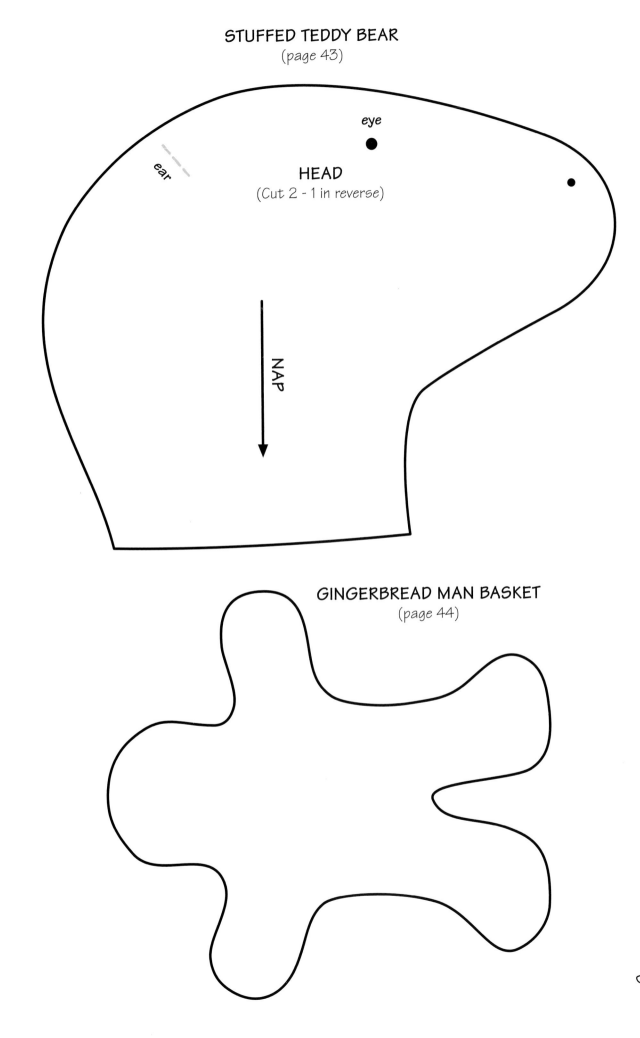

STUFFED TEDDY BEAR
(page 43)

eye

ear

HEAD
(Cut 2 - 1 in reverse)

NAP

GINGERBREAD MAN BASKET
(page 44)

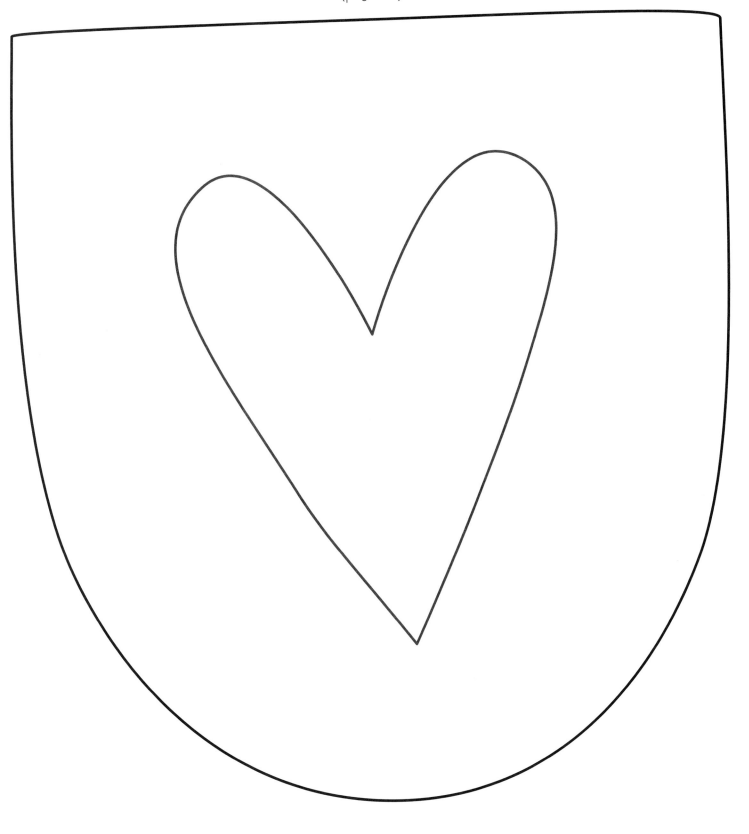

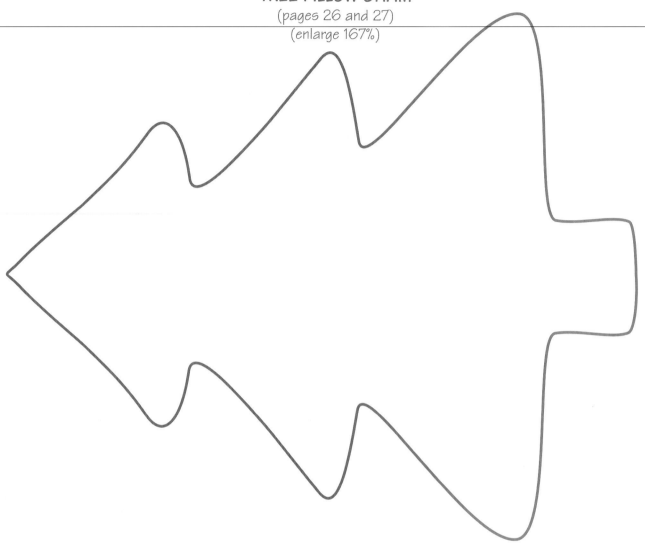

KITTY TREAT KEEPER
(page 71)

Kitty Treats

DOGGIE JACKET

(page 70)

(enlarge 200%)

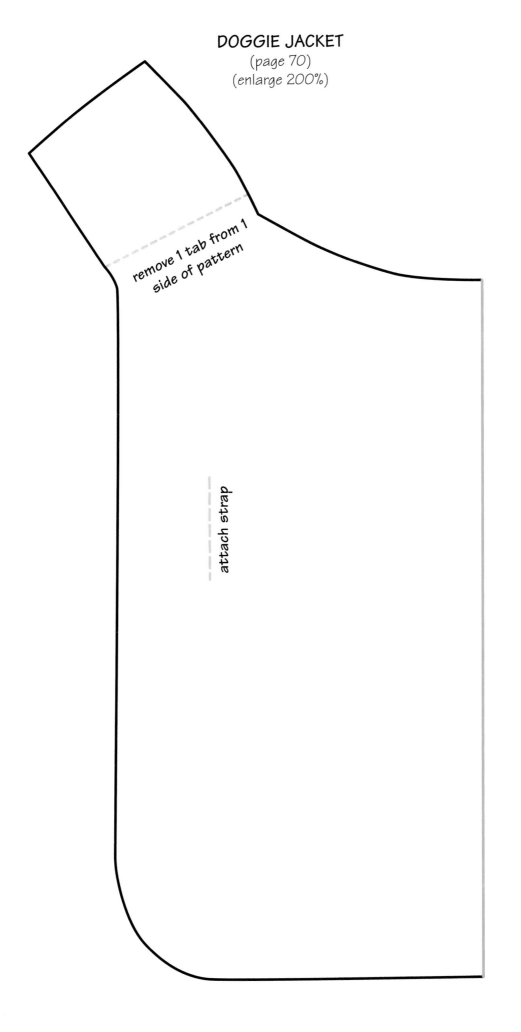

remove 1 tab from 1 side of pattern

attach strap

PROJECT INDEX

RECIPE INDEX